Bits of Wisdom

Nick-Anthony Zamucen

DEDICATION

The book is dedicated to my three children and beautiful bride. They are my greatest "Why" in this life. Gavin Michael, Cali Grace and London Marie, everything I do is for you and I love you all so much. Molly, you are truly an angel that has saved me more times then you know. At first glance I knew I'd love you forever. God has graced my life with far more then I deserve.

Only you can stop you, so never give up.

No one is ever proud of something that came easy.

(PS)

CONTENTS

INTRODUCTION

As I continue to live my life, reach new goals, and stumble over other ones, I find myself uncovering new business strategies, interpersonal skills, and life lessons. This book is a combination of all three. This is my third book that I've written and it is really a potpourri of sorts. My first book, *Flip It: The Real Book of Flipping Houses* was of course on real estate and it was written to be more of a how- to guide. My second book, *Bio-One Maverick Franchise* was about the franchise industry. Again, more of a how -to book and what to look for when buying a franchise. This book is more about life and how it affects your business and all business decisions.

My intent of this book is to help you reflect on your life, how you interpret your past and question how you see your future all in an effort to assist you in business. I have taken my years of personal development studies from my mentor Tony Robbins, and other like Jim Rohn, Brian Tracy and Jordan Belfort to name a few, who have helped me shape my thinking as an adult and business leader. With that being stated, my true belief is that life is what you make it. It is not your environment that shapes you, but rather it's your decisions, beliefs and the meaning that you place on your life events. Change can happen in a heartbeat once you have a big enough "Why." Anyone can change with the proper leverage.

I hope you read this book and decide that you are truly in control of your life. No matter where you come from, no matter what your story is, you, and you alone have control of your destiny. Start today to design your life, wakeup each morning with purpose and go to bed each night totally fulfilled. Life is beautiful so go live it to the fullest.

You Hold the Key.

Deep into the Mirror

Mirror: a reflective surface, now typically of glass coated with a metal amalgam, which reflects a clear image.

When you drive home today, you've got a big windshield on the front of your car. And you've got a little bitty rearview mirror. And the reason the windshield is so large and the rearview mirror is so small is because what's happened in your past is not near as important as what's in your future.
-Joel Osteen

This chapter is one that is very personal to me. From the title of the chapter, you may be asking, "Nick-

Anthony, what the does that mean, look deep into the mirror?" Well I am glad you asked, please continue reading, allow me to walk you over that bridge and show you where it leads.

I want you to make a promise, not to me, not to your spouse, or your parents, or your kids. I want you to promise you. Promise yourself that you are committed. It is truly an absolute "MUST" not just a "should" in order to improve the lives of you and your loved ones. Promise yourself that no one in your life now, no one in your past and certainly no one in your future will stop you from being the best person, business owner, parent, lover, scholar, athlete, writer, whatever you want to fill in the blank, no one will stop you from being your absolute best, no matter what. The bottom line is you owe you. Forget every excuse you have ever given to yourself, because it is truly just an excuse.

I believe if you are reading this book then you are better then any excuse you have given yourself in the past. The past is just that, the past. It means nothing for your future. You cannot change it, you cannot simply delete the past. The past has made you who you are up until now. Up until today, right this moment, you are going to write your future. You will no longer be trapped by the broken record that has been playing in your head about the past and who you are now. To be fair, I am not saying that your past has not influenced who you are today and how you think or make decisions. In all likelihood, if you are like most people, you've used your past for an excuse rather then a fire starter. If you are like most people you have been stuck in the quicksand of your past and it has hindered you, up until now.

Many people, and I mean many, blame their parents, blame how they grew up, blame their environment, blame whatever seems relevant to them at that time. By far the biggest excuse in todays American culture is the parents. "I blame my parents for not loving me enough, or for not being there for me or for smothering me." I can tell you that throughout my coaching career, I've heard it all. Maybe you did have a bad childhood, perhaps someone did not love you the way you wanted to be loved. There is a possibility that you had the worst childhood known to man, but I doubt it. Someone always had it worse, you just have not run into them yet. No matter how bad or good you had it, those facts of your life are just that, facts. They're facts not premonitions, not legitimate hindrances of your life today, they are just the facts. It's how you process those facts and the meaning that you put on past situations that predict the decisions

3

you make that directly affect your future. It is not your past alone which determines your future, it is the decisions you make that dictate who you are, why you do what you do and how your life will be.

Let's dive into my past, since I seem to be making the bold statements. I have been accused of growing up with a silver spoon in my mouth, or I must have had a privileged life. I would imagine people say that because of how I designed my life. They see the cars and the homes and vacations my family takes and think, "oh he must have come from money. He must have had it easy, what a charmed life he must have had". I am here to tell you, if I do have a charmed life, it is because I created it for myself. I certainly was not born into money and what some would call "success". The people that have accused me of this do not know me very well, or at all. They think from what they see, it must have just been smooth sailing. I'm here to tell you, life is what you make it, not where you come from.

I was born into a dysfunctional relationship from day one. To this day I have only seen my parents in the same space twice in my lifetime. Once at my high school graduation and the other when my sister was in the hospital before her untimely passing just a year ago. My sister Patience was anything but patient and she is part of my childhood history as well. Unfortunately, we didn't see eye to eye on life as adults. She looked and lived in the rearview mirror often and could not seem to part with her past as some of you cannot. Blaming gets us no where at any part of our lives.

My parents were young and we were on the road a lot in my early years because being a rock legend was my fathers dream, and my mom, sister and I as an infant were along for the ride. My mother was trying to raise two kids on the road with my father and the band, which caused some heartache, jealous moments, and some bad habits. My mother could only handle the road for about a year before she divorced my father a year after I was born. She moved us back to the mid-west where I spend a lot of my childhood years and she kept my father from my sister and I. I remember hearing my parents yell back and forth on the phone at each other often, it seemed to be a weekly event. My mother would position us against our father by handing us the phone and demanding we tell my father what was in our refrigerator. Normally, it was a package of opened hotdogs, week old tuna casserole, expired milk and some pickles. I remember this phone call specifically because when the call was over my mother screamed at me and my sister about how terrible my father was and how he didn't care enough to send us child support etc. My mother told me as a child that she would tell people white lies, because it was OK to lie if the lie did not hurt anyone. My mother was a very interesting lady.

My mother was a bit of an oxymoron. She would send us all to church on Sundays and play mom of the year in front of certain groups, but then would go party with her friends all weekend and leave my sister and I to fend for ourselves. So much so, it landed us in child protective services more than a handful of times. I remember when I was eight years old, child protective services came to the door and my sister and I had to convince the custody officer that our mother just ran to the store to buy groceries. The reality was that we had not seen her for a few days. The fact is that my mother was hooked on partying. This came with a lot of cocaine, alcohol, drunk driving, and many boyfriends. She was a bartender trying to raise two crazy kids as a single mom. She was not always single, she was married I believe five times. Four of those five by the time I was nine, so I had a lot of "fathers" in my life. The marriages never lasted very long, a year or so, then she went back to her old ways of being the life of the party and an absentee mother. My mother was young and extremely needy. She was a bit of a con artist as she could get almost anyone to believe her at anytime. She was not dumb, she just had no motivation and was always looking for the easy way out. My grandfather Vern would say she dated all the doctors and lawyers in town but married all the losers she partied with at the bar. "She always married all the wrong ones," he would preach.

I know what government cheese takes like. I know that food stamps come in a blue envelope with the two red strips once a month and what it is like to live in the back of a car. In fact, that's where I would sleep until the police would call child protective services and we would be placed either with a family member or foster care. My mother and her husbands would spank us with belts or homemade paddles and wash our mouths out with liquid soap until we gagged. Other times I was tied to the bed with pantyhose and belts so my mom could go party more. I wish I could say this was a one-time occurrence, but it was not. It happened more times then I could remember. I think about it now as a father and not only do I not spank my kids, but the idea of tying my child to the bed like a dog is absolutely insane. I couldn't move when I was strapped to the bed, what if there was a fire? I do remember halfway getting out, but just enough to crawl off my bed while still having my foot tied to the bed, so I slept with one leg in the air and the rest of my body on the ground. Perhaps I should have just stayed in my bed more and I wouldn't have gotten tied up? I write that with a little tongue-in-cheek, but no one said I wasn't stubborn.

My paradox as a child was as follows. I would go to church every Sunday, attend bible studies and vacation bible school every summer, but everything I learned in church was a complete contradicted at home. I was told at church do not lie, but I had my mother lying to everyone to get her way and manipulate situations to gain advantages. I was told to love thy neighbor but then I would watch my mom fighting with her friends and boyfriends and when I mean fighting, I mean physically fighting. To this day I can still hear in my head clear as day my mother being beaten in the other room and waiting for whichever boyfriend to come into my room to beat on me for a bit. I recall being seven years old and having one of my mothers boyfriends burn my wrist with a lit cigarette and tell me "tough guys don't cry and you better not tell your mom and if you do, I'll beat you the way I beat her, but worse." I still have that cigarette burn on my right wrist, it is a perfect circle of remembrance. For the record, I didn't cry nor did I tell my mother anything about it. I was scared, I was only seven, a year older then my son Gavin's age now. Can you imagine the type of coward who picks on a seven year old for defending his mother? I think that was the last time I was ever scared of anything or anyone. I do not write that to be tough or show you how cool of a kid I must have been. I mean, I was in fact a cool kid, but that is not the purpose of the story. I write it to tell of one of the many misfortunes of my childhood, and I have hundreds more like it.

I have stories of being beaten for not fighting a kid in the school yard who was three grades older then me. Beaten for not vacuuming with straight lines. Beaten for looking at someone the wrong way or lingering in the toy section too long knowing we could not afford toys. I had liquid soap squeezed in my mouth for using the Lords name in vein. I was backhanded for crushing the bread while carrying in the groceries. I was made to eat dinner until I threw up because I was accused of being wasteful with food. I had pepper put in my eye for speaking out of turn and questioning why my mother was saying those things about my father. Forced to eat hot sauce for spilling my milk. Choked unconscious for spending the quarters I had saved because my mother needed them for who knows what. I had to go to church on the church bus in my underwear because I could not find my slacks in time for the bus. To be fair, my mother did meet me at the church with my pants, but that was quite the bus ride. I was frequently slapped silly for getting dirty because we could not afford to do laundry again that week. I was even sexually molested by older girls whom my mother trusted and hired to watch my sister and I while she worked and spent the weekend away partying. Then I was called a liar by my mother when I told her about how the girls had made me touch them in places I didn't think I was suppose to and beaten for lying about the sexual assault. All of this happened to me while I was an unknowing nine year old boy.

Abandoning responsibility is nothing I take lightly. There were a number of times I would come home after school to my bags packed and sitting at the door because my mother could not handle raising a boy, and I was being shipped off to my father for the fourth time. After the fourth time, at the age of 12, I never went back to my mothers house. My sister stayed, and she and my mother had an unbreakable connection until the time of my sisters passing last year.

For the record, I do not write this out of sympathy or to seek for pity for my childhood, I write this out of fact. I write my history so that you know I have been through my share of pain, suffering and humiliation and I have learned through all of it, that no one should feel pain like I have. I know how bad life can seem in the moment. I know how easy it can be to blame others because of our past. To give yourself excuses because you were wronged in some way and you just can't, won't or don't really want to get over it. I do not know of anyone nor have I met too many people who have had a rougher childhood then me. I am sure they are out there, in fact I know they are, but I haven't met them. I am not saying this out of pride, I am saying it out of perspective.

I have every excuse in the world to be a drug addict, a drunk that walks around with a chip on my shoulder. No one would blame me if they knew the facts of my life. Quite frankly, people expect me to be a screw-up because of the way I was raised as a child. I still have people today when I run into them look at me sideways and say, in a condescending tone, how are you? How have you been? Did your mom ever get the help she needs? I remember how hard she was on you guys. I normally politely just tell the truth. All is great with me, I own several companies, have more than 300 employees that work for me, live in a beautiful custom home, I am completely debt free, make more than most doctors, professional athletes, and TV actors, my health is top notch, I have three beautiful children, a pageant wife and I am blessed to teach others the path to success from nothing. Overall I'm great, how are you? I don't spend a lot of time looking in the rearview mirror and neither should you. Again, you can't change a damn thing about the past. It's the past, never will be again, place it in a box and only bring it out when you can draw upon it for strength, not for anguish. The world is going to throw enough new challenges at you on a daily basis, there is no reason to continue looking in the past for validation of disappointment. Don't waste your time on that, you've got a life to design, the past is the past. Perhaps you should change the meaning of the past for you. Rather then regret and heartache, look at your past as a learning lesson. A lesson that was lived, beaten into you and now gratefully understood. Everyone has some source of reference for regret. How about turning that regret into a remembrance of what you don't want to do, what you don't want to ever be like again and a commitment or promise to yourself that you are greater then your past.

"Live everyday in an attitude of gratitude and your whole life changes."

-Tony Robbins

As far as we know, we only get one shot at this thing called life, the human experience. I believe that the soul is eternal, but the human part is very short, so why not make your years here as productive, profitable and as loving as they could be. Why settle for second or worse, third? Someone has to be the best, why not you? Are you still convinced that your past is controlling you or is the reason you act the way you do? Time to wake up, time to grow up. You owe it to yourself to be successful. You owe it to yourself to be better on a daily basis. Why are you going through life one day at a time with no purpose, why are you satisfied with that? If you're are not satisfied with your current life, then what are you doing to change it? What promises do you need to make? How long are you going to make excuses? How long are you willing to let yourself be let down, not by other people, not by society, not by politicians, not by the milkman, by you, you are letting yourself down. Stop it, now. Now is the time to make the changes, to make the promises. Now is the time to let your life be what it was meant to be.

Let me give you three quick tips on how to improve your life that I've learned by studying and being around my mentor, Tony Robbins:

1. <u>Live in an Attitude of Gratitude</u>

- If you spend time being thankful for what you have, the people in your life and live in a beautiful state of mind, your life changes. As a follower and friend I can tell you that this works. Be thankful for what you are, where you come from and how much you've grown. No more complaining about what you don't have. Think of it as what you don't have, yet.

2. Turn Your Expectations into Appreciations

- You have to understand that everyone thinks a bit differently and not everyone is a mind reader. It may seem normal to you to be upset when someone doesn't do something your way. If they didn't meet your expectations. They didn't follow your blueprint and now you're upset. Or even worse, are you constantly beating yourself up because life is not currently going as you planned? Are you upset that things just aren't working out and they seem to be for everyone else? That's called self -pity and that has to stop. Start appreciating your gift, where you are at in life and how far you have come. Appreciate your efforts and pat yourself and others on the back sometimes. Stop living as it is all black and white, there are many shades of gray.

3. Raise your Standards

- This is the one attribute that will immediately change the quality of your life. Raise your standards. Never again accept the status quo in your life. You have to decide that you are better then what you've been accepting and you will never again accept less. Raise the bar in your thoughts, your career, your relationships and most of all, raise the standards of your life.

Demand more for yourself than anyone could possibly expect. That is how I live my daily life and I employ you to do the same. You are in competition with yourself, so win and win big. I bet on myself everyday and so should you. Winning is a habit, it is something winners do. Winners win and losers lose. That may be a harsh way to say it, but it is true. Have you ever noticed that the same teams win week after week, month after month, and year after year. They have a certain standard for the team, for their players, for their business life. Why wouldn't you have that same demand of yourself? Can it be hard? Yes. Can it be frustrating? Yes. I am here to tell you that raising your standards and living life on your terms is worth every moment.

People are comparing themselves to you whether you know it or not. People are looking at you, wondering if you will pass or fail. The choice is yours on how they'll react towards you. Will you start to inspire them with your way of life, with your heightened self standards and your never give up attitude? Or, will you be someone the look to for amusement, a cautionary tale, someone who had all the promise but would not follow through because they were too busy looking for reasons why it wouldn't work rather then reasons it will. Either way, there will be an outcome. How do you want the story to be told?

You Hold the Key.

Always Purposeful

Purpose: The reason for which something is done or created or for which something exists.

"The meaning of life is to find your gift, the purpose of life is to give it away." -Pablo Picasso

I say this often in my daily life to people I coach, people who work for me, people I meet on the street, and just about anyone when I'm asked why I always seem to be so driven. I tell them, when I get out of bed each morning and my feet hit the ground, I want the devil to say, "shit, he's up!" Why do I do what I do? Why do my moves always seem planned and thought out, even the ones that come off as sporadic. Here's my answer: ***I am always Purposeful in my life.***

When I walk into a meeting or a social gathering, or even to have a beer with a buddy, I always have a result in mind. I'm purposeful about the event. If it's a business meeting, perhaps it's to close a deal or if I am with a friend maybe, it's just to have a good time and relax a bit. See, I know in advance what my goal or outcome for any planned situation and most unplanned ones because I've predetermined what I want out of the day.

Now, I'm not suggesting life is a series of planned moments every step of the way, but knowing your outcome makes your brain think and react differently to almost all situations to gain the original outcome. Does that make sense to you?

Let me give you an example:

Have you ever watched a politician speak or better yet, have you ever watched a presidential debate? Did you notice that when the person mediating the event, or trying to mediate the event, asks the politician a question the politicians always seems to answer the question they want to answer, not always the question they were asked. If their running platform is on Healthcare, then the mediator can ask a question about International Relations and the politician will somehow position their answer so that healthcare is brought into the answer. Or if they're running on a stronger military their answers will always circle back around to building the military. Do you think this is by accident? Or perhaps this type of spin is purposeful and planned out?

You have to decide to be purposeful in everything you do, in life, in business, in friendships. And, it is my not so humble opinion that if you're going to have a purpose, why not make your purpose to be great or even better. Be outstanding no matter what the situation.

When I get up every morning, I have a purpose for the day. It may be to get a large amount of work done so I can lead by example and better my company, or perhaps it is to spend time with my three kids and have an outrageous time doing so, so they feel loved and connected with me. Perhaps my day is spent shopping with my wife and making sure she has a great time and we have an amazing day together. Having a clear and excitable purpose in your life is a life certainly worth living, don't you agree? Did you happen to notice one thing when I write about purpose? It's not just the purpose, it's also about having a clear outcome for your purpose, your " what and why". It's not just spending time with my wife, it's spending time with my wife and having an amazing day together.

I've found in my years of business and in my life, having a purpose was an essential first step to happiness, but there needs to be an even larger motivating positive factor behind the purpose. What will the purpose bring to my life and why am I going to make sure it is congruent with my needs. The purpose in itself is selfish and that's fine if your outcome for the selfishness is bigger then you. Think of it as for the "Greater Good" in your life. Again, spending the day with my wife is something I selfishly like to do, for me. Making sure she has a great time is for her, and the all around amazing day is for us. Some people think that being selfish is a bad thing, I say that's complete nonsense.

Selfishness is a form of self-love. However, it can be abused just like anything in life can be, wouldn't you agree? Money, sex, experience, love, anything can be abused and taken advantage of. I could write an entire new book on those topics above, but for now, I'm going to take for granted that you have more then one reference to draw upon to agree with me that anything in life can be abused.

Let me explain my version of selfishness as I'm writing about it for this topic. You know when you are flying on a plane and the lovely flight attendants are going over their safety card and the oh so complicated floatation device that is conveniently under your seat in the unlikely event of a water evacuation. This is all excellent information, but the part I'm writing about is the next part the flight attendant normally says. They instruct you in the highly unlikely event of a pressure issue in the cabin, that you place your oxygen mask on before helping others. Interesting isn't it? They are saying, please be selfish at this traumatic, possibly life- ending, at best life -changing time, to help yourself first before helping others.

Put on your mask before trying to assist others, profoundly deep, even for the airlines. This is my exact point. You must take care of yourself before you can begin to show others the way. In the good book it says, "You shall love your neighbor as yourself. There is no other commandment greater than these." Those are true words written in the English Standard Bible. Mark 12:31 if you wish to look it up. The Man above himself tells us to love ourselves. No greater teacher than Him in my opinion, perhaps we need to listen more.

If we can all agree at this point that it is alright to be a little selfish with our own happiness, perhaps we should be purposefully practicing being happy on a daily basis. Maybe you should ask yourself a question. The question is, "What makes me happy? If I wanted to become happy right now and be in a state of happiness, not just for a moment, but all day, how would I do it?"

Being happy is a choice, just as being sad, mad, bothered, annoyed, angry, blissful, outrageous, regretful, thankful, or outstanding are all simply choices. No one, and I mean no one affects your emotions unless you choose or purposefully let them. Now some people would argue and say, "I was born this way, I can't help it." Or the one I like, "I'm Italian or Irish or Latin, we're just this way". Well, that's a cute little copout and extremely immature not to mention an extremely limiting way of controlling your life, but you can use it, doesn't bother me a bit. I don't believe if you're reading this book that you think or are saying those things very often, but I imagine you can think of someone who does. Why do we all know people like this? Why can almost everyone you know come up with a person who is a non-stop blamer or a non-stop worrier? Perhaps it is because society has rewarded that behavior more than once and continues to do so.

We all tend to stay around people who are like us or people who we think we would like to be like. Don't you think that's true? Test it. Think of someone you really like. Are they like you or are they like how you would like to be? We tend to reinforce our behaviors with similar or like-minded people. Now lets do the opposite, think of someone you don't like, I mean really can't stand. Are they like you or how you would like to be? My assumption if you're being honest with yourself, the answer is probably a resounding no. In our lives we consistently are looking for reinforcement and the proximity of those around you are some of the greatest influencers and reinforcements in your life. Regardless if it is right or wrong, good or bad those around you influence your thoughts, decisions, your actions and your state of mind. Perhaps you should take a look around you and do an inventory of the people you let influence you, and those around you in general. Are they helping your life? Meaning, are they adding value to your life on a daily basis or is it time to find a better source of connection with different people? You may be asking yourself, "Nick are you telling me to dump my friends?" If those friends are holding you back or not adding value to your life or adding value to those you love, then yes, dump them and do it now. Find a better group of people that suit your future and challenge you as a person. Be extremely purposeful about whom you let into your life and who is in your inner circle, because those that are close, will influence your choices, your actions and your life whether you like it or not. You better be wise about these choices and be extremely purposeful in these decisions.

Time is not a good indicator of a good friend. Just because they've "always been around" doesn't make them a good friend. Perhaps time has turned that person into a leech who is draining you of your "to-be" life. I am not saying that people are doing this intentionally or people are trying to harm you. What I am saying is that some good times and good memories should stay in the past and not unintentionally corrupt your future greatness. Sometimes you need to shed some scales in order to grow. Trying to drive a car while looking in the rear view mirror can be extremely dangerous. Not being purposeful about whom you spend time with and who you let in your inner circle could be just as dangerous. Love yourself and them enough to let them go so you both can grow and experience a higher quality of life then you can together living in the past. Again, if those around you aren't challenging you, lifting you up, making you see from a different point of view, then perhaps it's time for a proximity change.

To reiterate, it is not that these old friends or people you hang around with are bad people. I'm not saying that at all. What I am saying is that one of the largest indicators of how your life will turn out is from whom you spend time with. You, me, all of us tend to live up to the standards in which the people we spend the most time with expect and accept, bottom line. If one has low standards or questionable values I would assume most of the people they hang around with have similar thoughts about life and their values are congruent. I would again assume that that same people in that group live near one another, listen to similar music, watch similar shows on TV, and would agree on most social, practical, legal and political decisions. Challenge me on this if you like, but just take a look around. Society is split into groups for a reason and whether it is the country music scene or gangster rap, birds of a feather flock together. We tend to live up to the standards of those we surround ourselves with, good and bad. Be purposeful with your choices of friends because proximity is often overlooked and always underestimated in life.

What I find is that nowadays we are flooded with information, but what we are starving for is wisdom. With the internet, live streaming movies, mobile devices, non-stop 24 hour news stations all giving you information in one form or another but none are filling your day with purpose, meaning or a hint of wisdom. So we must seek out wisdom, we must guard our minds from what is unleashed on us daily, and we need you to strengthen your resolve in what's real, what truly matters and what's really important. Have a purpose for your life, a master plan or what I tell my clients in our coaching sessions, make sure you are creating your treasure map. The most basic way I can describe my feeling on purpose is if you're not intentionally, purposefully creating your master plan of life and setting your stage, your dancing on someone else's.

William Shakespeare writes, " All the world's a stage, And all the men and women merely players…." He wrote this in the late 1500's. This wisdom is timeless, there is nothing new about what I'm saying, but perhaps I just translate the message differently. Here's my thoughts on Shakespeare's writing, if all the world is a stage, then I want to be the one who built the stage, designed the entrances and exits and wrote the play which people of my choosing play as big of a part as I'd like them to. I want to design my life the way I want, not be randomly just a mere player in my life. Here's a little wisdom you may want to highlight and come back to. If you're not living your life with purpose and meaning, than I assure you, you are a part of someone else's plan. Merely just a player in their story. We all fit somewhere, somehow, there is a plan for all of us. I also believe that we have freedom of choice and we can choose to create and design the life we've always dreamed of or we can just be a drone and be directed what to do for the rest of our lives. If you choose to not live with purpose, to make no conscious daily decisions about your life, don't worry, someone else will and hopefully you'll like their vision.

This is why most people go through life working a nine to five job, are under paid and under valued seemingly emotionally broke, spiritually broke, mentally spent and just unhappy with the results they're getting from life. Have you ever felt that way? Perhaps you should heed my words and begin today to design your life, begin to build that stage and direct your life instead of playing a part in someone else's design. In The King James Bible Proverbs 29:18 "Where there is no vision, the people parish..." Do you have vision, do you live with purpose or are you set to play a role or parish in someone else's design for you? Don't be merely a player, use the wisdom that is all around you, seek and you shall find, ask and you shall receive. I believe the Lord wants you to take action upon your life, He says it many times in the Bible. Living with purpose and grit are some of the gifts our Creator has given to us, don't waste them because you don't see or act upon them. You are reading this book for a reason, whatever that reason, it is personal to only you. Perhaps this is an intentional wakeup call, a call to live with purpose and start designing your life today.

It's not our environment, which dictates our lives, it's the decisions we make. There are so many examples of greatness coming from less than ideal situations. In turn, there are so many examples of massive failure when everything was handed to someone and they never had to make any decisions. Why do some people that come from nothing, with every disadvantage life can throw at them still manage to be wildly successful? Because those people purposefully chose to be greater then their environment. They designed their life rather then being a victim of their circumstances. They made the hard choices and learned what wasn't easily taught. They demanded more from their life then what was offered. They were purposefully great and now reap the rewards. My strong belief is this, if you were born in America poor it's not your fault, but if you die poor, that is all on you. Live with purpose and design greatness, anything less is wasteful.

As you read and are hopefully learning, being purposeful makes you have to evaluate life in many ways. I hope you didn't pick up this book thinking I was full of positivity and rainbows, that is not me. I'm also not all gloom and doom. I am the guy who you come to for truth and the sometimes harsh realities of life. I share with you my thoughts out of love for people and to assist you in making your life as great as you want it to be. A friend is someone who tells you "things will be OK, just stay the course and it will all workout", that's why I'm not your friend. I'm your best friend, the one that tells you things are messed up, this has gone way too far and you need to change because your life needs help. Good news is, I'm here to help. I do not wallow in self-pity nor will I allow you to. Not on my watch, I'm here to advance you, help get you where you want to go and show you a life your old self could only dream of, and your future self will thank you for. Why, because I'm your best friend and you owe it to you, not me. I want for you Champagne to fall from the heavens, all the doors to open and velvet ropes to part. Why shouldn't you have all you have ever desired? Who's telling you no besides the bullshit story you made up in your head. Let's change that story into one of total fulfillment and a love for life you only imagined.

See, no matter what you do if you have a strong enough purpose and compelling reasons for that purpose, the outcomes are almost predestined. This is why I always seem to know the outcome, or why it seems I can read people so fast. When you set the table before anyone has even received an invite to dinner, you always know where the butter is. Know your outcome, control your destiny.

"The purpose of life is not to be happy. It is to be useful, to be honorable, to be compassionate, to have it make some difference that you have lived and lived well."
- Ralph Waldo Emerson

You Hold the Key.

No One Cares

Mickey Mantle? That's what you're upset about? Mantle makes $100,000 a year. How much does your father make? If your father can't pay the rent go ask Mickey Mantle and see what he tells you. Mickey Mantle don't care about you. Why should you care about him? Nobody cares.

-Sonny, A Bronx Tale 1993

A very sad fact of life but a very true fact of life is that your family and friends are usually the biggest dream killers. The same people you turn to for support and encouragement of your dream, are the same ones who normally kill it. They don't care about your dream the way you do. The bank doesn't care about your dream. Your neighbor doesn't care about your dream. The man on the corner begging for money doesn't care about your dreams. No one cares, so stop thinking that will change when you begin to become more successful.

I used to think that when I became a millionaire my life would change and everything would seem easy, because I had money. Do you ever have that thought? The thought is wrong, life doesn't work that way. I work harder now then I did when I didn't have money. I don't work for money now, I work for results. I have goals and a vision for my company. I design my life so it doesn't matter how much money I have or don't have. It's not about the money, it's about the results. Does anyone care I'm a millionaire? No. Should you care? No. Why would you? You should care about you and your bank account, not mine. Focusing on me will get you nowhere.

You have to focus on you, your dreams, your desires, your visions and your life design. See, no one cares about you more then you, so stop complaining. No more blaming the past. No more blaming your parents. No more blaming what could have been, should have been and whose fault it is. Let me tell you, your problems are probably your fault in one way or another. I'm not trying to upset you, I'm just being real with you. We all design life in the way we choose. If you don't proactively choose then that's a choice too. If your life isn't where you want it to be, then change it. Yes, it sounds simplistic, but it is very easy to change. Change isn't hard, it doesn't take days or months or years to change. Change happens in an instant, once you have enough leverage, but more on that later. Let me remind you, no one cares about your excuses, no one cares about the bullshit story you are telling to yourself at night so you can sleep. No one cares about your success or lack thereof. You should care, you need to change for you. You need to change for your future, for your life, because no one is going to do it for you. No one cares like you do, nor should they.

I have found in life people change for one of two reasons, either inspiration or desperation. Think about it, when you had to make a major life change, was it because something inspired you? Inspiration can be set in a positive notion or negative setting. You can be inspired by a child who looks at you and says, "Mommy please stop smoking because I don't want you to die. I want you to help me plan my wedding one of these days." You could be inspired by seeing someone on television who lost 300lbs and it inspires you to lose those 10 vanity pounds. Or, how about being inspired by reading your favorite Bible verse or watching your favorite fight scene in a movie, or perhaps listening to your favorite song.

Inspiration is everywhere. There are so many places we

can go to for inspiration now a days. It's easier then ever in the age we live in. For God's sake, it's not the information age anymore, it is the entertainment age, so go find inspiration from entertainment. I've always found my biggest inspiration is through my family. I have three beautiful children who are all sharp as a tack. I'm inspired by their love and curiosity, not to mention their abundance of nonstop energy. I'm not yet a billionaire, but I would be if I could figure out how to bottle their energy.

Then there is the other side of the coin. Changing out of desperation. Have you ever had to do this? I find more people change out of desperation then anything else, sad but true. People find themselves making a radical change when the doctor says, "You're going to have a heart attack and likely die if you don't lose the weight, or don't stop smoking, or don't start exercising." Have you ever had the crap scared out of you into doing something? Making a change because if you didn't, there are some pretty serious consequences coming your way.

People can always rationalize why they do not change even when they know they need to. If you don't like what is going on in your life or relationship, you can always go to the past when it was good or acceptable and wish it could be like that again. Or you can go to the future and think up whatever you want to make you feel better because it is the unknown. I find that God has a funny way of stepping in and making us change when we need it. Have you ever experienced anything that scared you so much that you said, "I have to change now, because if I don't my life is over!" Have you ever gotten to that point, perhaps in a relationship when you said, it's over, it was lousy in the past, I'm unhappy now and this will not get any better in the future, I am done with this! You may have done this with a job or a personal relationship or even something like overeating or smoking. You made a change because you where so desperate to get out of the situation, that was the leverage you needed to move on.

I had a good friend of mine, who when he reads this story will know it is about him, say to me, "Nick I am sick of everything! I'm sick of my living situation, I hate my financial situation, I am so irritated most nights I sleep like crap. I'm arguing with my wife non-stop every night, I'm short with the kids and I even look at the dog and I want to kick it sometimes! I'm just so damn sick of it all." So I looked at him very excitedly and with great enthusiasm sad, "That's great man! Congratulations!" then I sat there with a silly grin on my face. He looked at me and said, "What? Did you just hear what I said? I said I basically hate my life." I said, "Basically? It sounds like it is all bad. Nothing is going right, it just all sucks and I think that's great!" Now, I was not trying to be mean to my friend or make fun of his situation because he was in pain. He came to me for help or maybe just a shoulder to cry on, and I gave him something completely unexpected.

As he stood there and looked at me with his mouth wide open and a glazed look of pure confusion on his face, I continued to explain my beliefs. I said, "Man that is great news for you, it means you are about to make a change. Your life is about to change and you are about to make some big decisions." I told him that people only change for two reasons, inspiration or desperation, and he sure seemed desperate, shamefully, desperate. I like to rile my friends a bit and he knew I was saying it out of love and respect, not poking fun. To be fair, I was happy he was in this spot, because I knew for a while he was not happy, but you can't help someone who doesn't want to help themselves. When they do decide its time, change is hard so you need major leverage to help in that change. I knew I had the leverage I needed to help him through a major life change. He needed a perspective shift. He was focusing on what was wrong with his life instead of focusing on what was right.

It is always easier to focus on what is wrong with a situation. That is just how our brains work. Look for the problem so we can find a solution. Ever heard of the saying, "If it seems too good to be true, it probably is?"

Now that is a pretty pessimistic way of going through life. It reinforces us to look for the bad rather than looking for the good, and we wonder why no one cares. It is a pretty simple concept, if you are always looking for something bad, you'll find it. On a beautiful sunny day, there is always someone worried about getting a sunburn or complaining about the glare on their car windshield. Now that the sun is out the grass will start to grow and pollen will soon fill the air and millions of people will get allergies. The mornings get lighter sooner and the birds start chirping earlier and waking you up. Man, there is so much negativity to focus on if we want to.

I wrote a few of those obviously with sarcasm but some people really do focus on the most negative part of life and they seem to live there. Do you know anyone like this? How do you feel when you are around people like this? Ever just feel like smacking them and saying, stop complaining! It is a beautiful day! Now, I am not actually asking you to go around and start smacking that person you are thing of, but what I am saying is that you can always find what you are looking for, if you focus on it.

Matthew 7:7 (NIV) *Ask and it will be given to you; seek and you will find; knock and the door will be opened to you.*

We find whatever it is we are looking for. This is the same to be true when looking for something good. We can always find something good in a situation. Perhaps it is not good in the moment, but it will lead to something good. The situation may lead to a new life, or new empowering understanding or belief structure, who knows. What I do know is there is light even in the darkest time. You just have to be willing to look for it and receive it. Here is a great thing I heard from Tony Robbins and I want you to adopt this belief system. "Life is happening for you, not to you." I believe that everything in life is here to serve you in one-way or another. It is either here to strengthen you or open your eyes, perhaps show you a new meaning or assist you in serving someone else. Nothing is perfect, no doubt about that, but we choose where to focus our intention on. This mindset of choosing to look for good rather than bad is a necessary part of growth and getting what you want out of life.

When I say no one cares, I don't mean no one cares about you. People love and respect you, I don't have any doubt about that. They do not care about your dreams the way you do. Choosing your future, by choosing what you focus on and intentionally designing your life is necessary to your desired outcome. No one cares as much as you do about your success, your dreams, your goals or your long term vision and life design. You must work on yourself daily, grow and expand your mind. You must, what I call "live by the principle of NWT". No Wasted

Time. No Wasted Time means you respect your life and your future so much that you are not willing to sacrifice your time wasted on things and people that don't help you to your goals. You surround yourself with people of valor and who will challenge you to do better and to be better. Be around people who have similar and hopefully higher standards for you then you do. People who will not let you get away with being lazy, not pulling your weight, or not giving your all. People who will not let you just be average, because average sucks.

Do you know that the average American household still watches television 35 plus hours a week? This doesn't even include being on the computer, just watching the television. Did you know that the average American makes roughly $42,000 a year, lives in a home less than1800 square feet, drives a car worth less then $15,000, has saved less then $100,000 for retirement and has more then $23,000 in debt? Lets look at more stats of the average American. They are more them 15 lbs over weight, eat fast food 4 times a week, drink 42 gallons of soda a year and say that their best days are far behind them. What kind of future do you think the average American is working towards? Still think it is OK to be average. Still feel like settling to be like everyone else? So no one cares because being average has been socially acceptable. Having a mediocre quality of life is what is expected. Why do you need more? Do you think you are better than that? I sure hope you do. I hope it is a resounding YES! Yes I want more for my life, my family, my friends and those around me. I hope you wont settle for just being average, because the average American is not happy, is not fulfilled and has lost their dream somewhere along the way. Fight like hell for yours, because no one is betting on you to get it. In fact, they are most likely betting in the other direction, betting that you'll lose. Not because they don't care about you, but because they do care about you and don't want to see you get your hopes and dreams crushed. Perhaps they don't want you to succeed because of their own insecurities, because if you make it, then why didn't they? I'll tell you. They didn't have a big enough WHY, and they gave up.

Mediocrity sucks and it is not fulfilling. You need to have a big enough WHY you MUST, not should but MUST obtain your life goals. What is a big enough why you ask? It is different for everyone. For me, it's my kids and my wife. I don't want my kids to ever know the way I grew up. I don't want them to know what it feels like to have a free lunch voucher in school when everyone else has to pay for their hot lunch, and get made fun of because of the free card. I do not want them to ever have to worry about their friends seeing them in the store while mom uses food stamps. Or have people at their school laugh at them for wearing knockoff Nike's or last years styled jeans. I don't want them to steal other kids lunch money and fight on the playground to stand up for themselves. Children should never know what it's like to live in a car during a snowy winter and mom can't turn the car on for warmth because she's scared of running out of gas. I never want them to be scared because they heard a knock on the door thinking it was child protective services to take them away again or maybe the knock is landlord kicking everyone out because mom didn't make rent again. Kids shouldn't know what government cheese tastes like and how to make powdered milk for cereal. They shouldn't have to go to their friend's house after school in hopes of stealing a few slices of bread from their pantry. I did, and I put it in my borrowed baseball glove so I could eat it in the outfield without anyone seeing. I was so hungry because I hadn't eaten that day. I could go on and on, but my WHY is very clear and very strong. My kids will never grow up the way I did. Do you have strong enough emotional anchors of your WHY?

Let me end the chapter like this. One of these days, you're going to die. We get one shot at this thing called life and the goal is to play the hand you were dealt like it was the hand you wanted. Stop giving yourself damn excuses of why you can't do this or that, or who is stopping you. You are just bull-shitting yourself so you feel better about why you don't have what you want or why your life is not what you hoped for. It is all on you, no one cares as much as you do. They've all got their own shit in life, they don't have time for yours. They are too busy making their own excuses and pacifying their own emotions. They don't want to think that you're doing better then them. Let me tell you the truth, because I assume that is why you are reading this book. They secretly do not want you to be successful. Why? Because in this self-serving mediocre world you have created until now, people are self-serving and looking to make themselves feel better by watching you fall.

There are two ways to have the biggest building in town, build it or tear everyone else's down. Most people do the latter, they tear down the next guys building because it is too damn hard to build one of their own. That's much easier and quicker after all. People do not care about how much work and effort it took to build the building, it makes them feel inferior and insignificant, so better to just tear it down. It would be just too much work to build one of their own, so get the bulldozers and smash it to pieces. If you have a dream you have to protect it, season it and massage it until it becomes your reality. And when it is reality, it's not over, it's just begun because you'll always been growing, caring and nurturing that lifestyle. I would love to be able to say it gets easier, but hey, that's not life. Some aspects are easier, I'm no longer worried about money or how much things cost. I pretty much do what I want, when I want with whom I want.

I've done a pretty good job of designing my life that way. But, I still work harder then anyone I know, even now it is 2:24am and I'm writing this book after being at my office with my employees for 10 hours and working from home for the last six hours.

See in my life I have a standard, a standard for family life, my work life and myself. I choose to work as much as I do, no one makes me. That is who I am because that is who I choose to be. See we choose which path we want to take, no one chooses it for you. You can blame certain circumstances or life cycles on why you are where you are, but again you're just looking to blame someone for your choices and you are only fooling yourself. Trust me on this one, no one cares.

If you want something, go get it. End of story.

"Never apologize for having high standards. People who really want to be in your life will rise up to meet them." --Anonymous

You Hold the Key.

Evolving Leadership

"Victory has a hundred fathers and defeat is an orphan."

-John F. Kennedy

It seems to me that everyone wants to be a leader, or certainly likes the idea of being one. When you are a young boy, we all wanted to be the quarterback in the fourth quarter of the Super Bowl when your team was down by six and you needed to lead the offense to the winning touchdown. Perhaps we wanted to be the pitcher in the bottom of the ninth of game seven in the World Series. See we all wanted to be the one in charge, the hero of the story. What happened? Did you become that leader, that hero? Do you look at yourself in the mirror daily and see a winner, a leader? Did you make it where you think you would or have your leadership qualities been tampered down a bit due in part to everyday life? How is the "grown -up" responsible world that you live in today, making a living just get by? Is this fulfilling your soul, the inner child, or do you sometime, or maybe all the time, feel like you are just spinning your wheels in Georgia Red Clay?

Some people say that leaders are born and not made. I do not believe that at all. What that would mean is that if you did not hit the lottery of life and lucky enough to be born a leader, then you have no chance. That thinking seems a bit short sided and unrealistic to me. My thoughts are that most people are born with some leadership qualities, but not everyone advances the qualities, not everyone hones the skills of leadership. When I see a child who seems a bit bossy and usually ornery to his parents I laugh and tell the parents, "Congratulations, your child has strong leadership qualities. I hope you put them to good use, they could use those qualities in the White House."

I believe that great men and women are not born great, that are made to grow great. With that being stated, have you been practicing being great? Is being great part of your daily life? If not, why? Do you have a lack of reasons to be great? Do you have the lack of resources to be great? I have always found that being great started in the mind and was portrayed with consistent actions. Being great is a habit, not an exception. When was the last time you were great? Do you remember the last time you felt that sense of pride, that sense of, "Yes, I did that, it was me." Being great will only give you momentary feelings. You need to practice being great, better yet, perhaps you should practice being outstanding. To stand out of the crowd, even in the crowd of those around you who may be great. Great will always look up to outstanding.

Let me give you an example of what I call notching up. I heard this said to me years ago and I don't remember who said it or came up with it, but I do know it stuck with me for many years now.

When you do a poor job, what kind of results do you get? Poor right? No, you don't get poor results when you do poorly, you get little to no results. The universe is not tit-for-tat like some like to think it is. The house always has the advantage, you never get a like-for-like situation in life. So let's move on. When you do a good job what are your typical results? Good? Nope, you get poor results. Yes that is correct, when you are just good at something you get poor results. Good is rarely good enough.

When a parent or a athlete comes to me and says "I'm a good parent" or "I'm a good athlete, why did I get cut, why do my kids not like me. Why have I lost connection?" Here is why, and read this closely. Being good is not good enough. Being good gets you poor results. You can not afford to be a just a good parent, just a good husband or wife, just a good athlete. Good will only give you poor results, so being good, again, is not good enough. A good husband leads you to a life of unfulfilled dreams. It does not seem fair does it? I know, I agree, but you let me know where the to ticket booth is to the life is fair and I'll buy all the tickets up. Fair is not the issue nor is it reality. Fair should not be something you are thinking about, what you need to think about is how do I become great.

Being great is not a bad place to be, but being great will only lead you to good results. Does that not really make you mad? Being great means you only get good results. You know if you really want to yield all the fruits of your labor, if you really want the good life you need to jump to the next level. You need to level up and the time is now. You need to become outstanding. You should be practicing the art of being outstanding. Be an outstanding parent, an outstanding husband or wife, be an outstanding business owner, outstanding partner, whatever you want comes a bit easier when you are living an outstanding life. Becoming outstanding is practiced. You need to consciously be outstanding at everything you do. Here is the magnificent thing about becoming outstanding, it is just a few little clicks above great.

See the difference between poor and good is a huge leap. Just as being good to great is an equally large leap, but to be outstanding from great, just takes a small little effort. Outstanding is where all the rewards you deserve and crave are. If you really want to be a true leader, a leader in your community, in your relationships, in your business, in your life, then you must be outstanding in everything you do. Does it take effort, yes of course it does. Let me give you a tip though, no one is ever proud of something that was easy. Why? Because it was easy so there is nothing to be proud of.

Think of every strong leader you can think of, are they outstanding at what they do? To be a strong leader you have to be outstanding, there is no way around it. Few people will put in the work to be outstanding so that is why those that are stick out so much.

Outstanding, again starts in the mind and is repeated in actions. It is an art, a skill that is developed, carved like a samurai blade. The samurai blade is made with perfect precision, down to ounce per centimeter.

The sword was a very elegant weapon in the days of the samurai. You had honor and chivalry much like the knights, and yet it was a gruesome and horrific weapon.

-Dustin Diamond

Here are nine traits in leadership:

1. Think systemically and act long term.
Outstanding leaders achieve results through a combination of systemic thinking
and acting for the long term benefit of their organization. They recognize the interconnected nature of the organization and therefore act carefully. Think twice act once.

2. Bring meaning to life.
Outstanding leadership enables a strong and shared sense of purpose across the organization. They emphasize emotional connection for people with a

focus on passion and on ethical purpose. Vision is greater then one idea, man or concept.

3. Apply the spirit not the letter of the law.
Outstanding leadership focuses on the few key systems and processes which help provide clarity, give structure, enable feedback, give time for discussion and enable the development of vision. They use them to achieve outcomes rather than focus on the process and put flexibility and humanity first.

4. Grow people through performance.
Outstanding leaders passionately and constantly invest in their people and use the challenges presented every single day to encourage growth, learning and engagement. Not everyone is motivated the way you are, so study your employees, co-workers and loved ones in your life.

5. Leaders are self-aware and authentic to leadership first, their own needs second.
Outstanding leaders unite a deep understanding of others, high levels of self-awareness and a systemic appreciation of their symbolic position to become a role model for others.

6. Understand that talk is work.
Outstanding leadership depends on trusting and positive relationships that are built over time for the

long-term benefit of the people and their organization. They spend huge amounts of time talking with people to understand what motivates and how they can support and enthuse others. When you know everyone, everyone feels heard on issues big and small. Don't forget, you may not always have the best answer to the challenge.

7. Give time and space to others.
Outstanding leaders both give significantly more time to people than non-outstanding leaders and allow their people considerably more freedom and influence over the work they do and how they do it. The bottom line for me is that no one wants or likes to be micromanaged. Hire the talent and let them do their job.

8. Put 'we' before 'me'
Outstanding leaders work hard on issues such as team spirit, shared decision making, collaborative working and a strong bond within and between teams. Sustainable performance comes from collective wisdom and intent, encouraging people to get involved, and giving them voice and autonomy.

9. Take deeper breaths and hold them longer.
Outstanding leaders actively build trust by delivering on promises and acting with consistency, which in turn, leads to a sense of security and greater freedom

of expression. They understand the power of trust to speed up interactions, enable people to take risks, diminish arguments and disputes and reinforce innovation.

Everyone wants to be the boss until it is time to write a check. Here is what I find kills most business owners. They feel controlling the purse string and keeping people in the dark about financials is somehow helping their business. They act as if the employee has no idea of what they charge or they should not know what they charge. Why is this? Well, in my opinion they are worried about the employee demanding more money because of what the job is being charged. It is a very immature way of running a company. In one of my franchised organizations I own, they sell franchises for around $85,000. Everyone in my company knows this, everyone is OK with this and very few of them are making $85,000 a year on salary. That companies sells roughly 25-50 franchises a year. Doing the quick simple math, that means the company takes in 2 million to 4 million per year just off franchise fees. This number does not count ongoing royalties from each franchise. Question, do you think I am paying even anyone $500,000 a year? The answer is a resounding no. Most people who work in that franchise organization know the numbers, and they also know if they want to make

more, they better add more value. We pay people for
what they are worth, not for what we feel is fair or
industry standards. We have appointment bookers at
one of my companies making up to $100,000 a year
and executives at another making $85,000. Again, we
pay what your value is, not what industry says. Here
is the great thing, you can literally earn what you want
with me, and you just have to show me value.

See hiding the numbers from people and treating them
like children does not make a better employee. I
believe saying to them, you see the numbers, and you
want a bigger piece of the pie, well then work for it.
Show me that you can be outstanding, show me that
you are worth to us what you feel you are.

As a leader you have to show a vision greater then
them. People want to feel apart of something greater,
something to be proud of, something to talk about at
family gatherings. If you can bring someone in on a
vision and make them feel like it is their vision too,
then you have a great company. To give someone the
ability to believe in something great, what I call the
"greater good" this can change their entire outlook on
life. Show them where they fit in, in this equation and
make them understand that they are a part of it. People
like to know not only where they fit in, but that they

do, in fact fit in.

I own a company where the people in it, willingly go get a tattoo of the company mark. Have you ever heard of that? Yes, people that are in one of my companies have branded their body for the rest of their life with our company logo. Talk about some company culture, talk about having strong leadership, and talk about having the right people in the system. That is something I am very proud of. I am so proud of the guys we have working for us in this particular franchised company, we are truly a family and I am honored to be the head of it.

Here is an example of great to outstanding. The England Rugby League player Sam Burgess showed outstanding leadership in the recent Australian Grand Final. In the first few minutes of the final Sam Burgess fractured his cheekbone and his eye socket, but not only did he stay on the field, but he played on and won the man of the match as he led South Sydney to victory.

This is a great role model, leading by example, leading your troops from the front, and showing them what being a winner is all about.

Imagine the trust that has now been built up between him and his fellow players. They know that the can completely rely on him no matter what happens.

When people show this type of leadership, especially in sports, it can have a tremendous impact on the overall squad as they know that they have a leader that they can follow and look to emulate, and when everyone in the team follows that lead it changes the whole character of the team.

Sam is not the first player to have played on in spite of such injuries, there have been several others who have done similar things and all of them went on to become legends of the game. It's amazing the impact it can have when you have a legend in your team, not just on your own players, but also on the opposition too, who may become in awe of such a player.

I have seen Sam play several times and it does not surprise me that this happened, he has always been a 110% player, someone the team could rely on, and given the position he played he always led the charge from the front.

It will be interesting to see what happens now if he switches sports to play rugby union, and looks to be part of the England team which will challenge for the World Cup next year.

I know it will be a different game for him, and this injury might cut short his preparation time, but he will now arrive with a fearsome reputation, as a legend of rugby league, which will definitely inspire his own team mates and possibly put a bit of fear into the opposition.

Inspiring Leaders can come in all shapes and sizes, some inspire through their words, others through their intellect and planning, and some by the examples that they set.

A leader is one who knows the way, goes the way, and shows the way.
-John C. Maxwell

You Hold the Key.

Free Your Mind

*"What if every problem and pain you had was **life happening for you – not to you**? If you master meaning, you master life."* –Anthony Robbins

This phrase above was said to me right before I took the stage when speaking at a seminar with over 6,700 raving fans. It's profound and deep if you simply dissect the sentence. Tony (Anthony) asked me, "what if everything in life was happening for me, not to me?" At first you could read those few sentences and say, "how absurd" or "complete psychobabble mumbo jumbo." It is easy to dismiss, but hard to forget once you've thought about it. What IF everything in life, good and bad was happening for me, not to me? IF you were to believe that statement and IF you were to accept that this is true, then how would that belief system impact your life? Would you look at things a bit different? Would you look back and wished you had treated some people or behaved in a situation differently?

To free your mind is simply a choice to believe in a better meaning. To not think like a victim of your circumstances and start questioning, what if it was all for a reason, to better you, to make your grow? Let me ask you something. Can you think of a time in your life that seemed so painful, seemed like total desperation, there was no way out, no correct answers, the world was caving in on you? Then a few hours went by, maybe a few days or weeks, perhaps a few years and you looked back at that what seemed to be a tragic event, the one that was going to kill you and the one you thought you could never come back from and suddenly you realized, it was the best thing to ever happen to you? What seemed like the end of the world was just the beginning of a better, stronger, more employing life? Can you think of a time like that in your history?

Perhaps it was a business failure or a divorce. Maybe it was being late to a meeting and getting scorned or forgetting to take the dog out? See whatever this "terrible" event was in your life probably helped you in one way or another. Perhaps you were too quick to judge the outcome and thought the story had ended when a new one was just beginning. Haven't you experienced what

I'm writing about in your own life, maybe more than once?

What I find is that people are so quick to run negative patterns in their minds and miss what's about to happen. Perhaps the breakdown was really a breakthrough. As you look back on certain events in your life, can you find some references that were actually a blessing in disguise? Something that seems so bad today could be the break you were actually waiting for. Perhaps we all have been taught to react a little to quick and think a bit to short sided. When we think a negative thing happens, it may actually just be the best part of this year or even your life.

Let me give you an example, a personal one many of you may not know. I was dating this lovely little Welsh woman for five years. Now, while we loved in the United States, she frequently traveled back to the Wales and London, England to visit her family, while I stayed back in the States to work. Let's call her Chelsea for the purpose of this story. Chelsea had retuned to our home after a three week visit back to the U.K. and seemed exceptionally quiet for a few days. I thought perhaps she was just tired and needed some time to acclimate back to our time zone. After all, it was an eight hour time difference between the U.K. and California. A few more days passed and still, Chelsea was very quiet and when she did speak, it was short just to the point. Red flags were everywhere now and I thought we should go to dinner and have a proper chat.

While we were at dinner she confessed to me that she missed her family and home back in the U.K. and wanted "us" to move back. Unfortunate as it may seem, I was in the middle of a business deal that had been taking most of my time for a stretch of a year, but also didn't see the point in losing her. I told her to move back to the U.K. and I'll shortly follow. As we packed her stuff in the next few weeks, Chelsea almost seemed to resent going back without me. Mind you this was a clear conversation and thought-out approach to making her happy. I was excited at the thought of living overseas and even went into business with a friend of mine who was a professional soccer player in Manchester, England. As I took her to the airport for her final flight home, she was a mess. She thought it was such a terrible idea that she was going without me, that if I didn't board the plane with her right then and there we were over. I tried to calm her down and said I would be over as soon as I wrapped up some business in Arizona and New York.

Well, a few months passed and we spoke less and less. Then a year passed and I would only hear about her in the pub I owned, asking about me and soon she was seen with other "blokes" around town. When I heard about this I wasn't surprised, it had been a year and we hadn't seen each other more then two or three times, but I was still hurt a bit. After all, we never officially ended our relationship, we never formally said it was over. But, then again we did live 5,300 miles away from each other. I still didn't feel right about it, she was in my pub with another guy and I heard about it second hand. I was getting pretty worked up about this over the next several days. It didn't feel right and I had made some hasty moves to close those deals I was working on and decided I was going to head over to the U.K. and win her back. After all, I couldn't just throw five years away and six if you count the year she lived there without me. I had to be a man and do what men do, I must go over there and show some American muscle.

There was one last dinner I had to attend with what would soon be my ex -business partners here in the States and as I sat at the bar waiting, to my left a group of women walked in and sat in a booth looking like they were just finishing their day and needed a drink to unwind. I didn't pay much attention because I was on a mission to finalize this deal and catch a plane in a few days to the U.K. I had major life issues to attend to. To my eyes pleasure, in walked a tall beautiful blonde that seemed to show up fashionably late to her friends. My eyes could barely leave her and I had to know who this woman was. There were seven girls squished into a round booth and the one I wanted to speak with was of course in the middle of all them. How does one gain attention of that one in the middle of six others? You simply buy them all drinks, and I did.

After the lovely cocktail waitress gave them all their drinks and pointed over to me across the room, I decided now's the time. I strolled over to the table of seven and said in my coolest of cool Jack Nicholson voice, "now that you all have something to wrap your lips around for a few minutes, I'd love to talk to you for a minute" as I pointed to the girl in the middle. Well, a few minutes turned into a few hours and then a few days and at this point seven years, three beautiful children, and more daily happiness then I ever thought was possible. Needless to say, I never made that flight to the U.K. and I never thought about Chelsea ever again. Molly, my wife, is the only woman I think about and try to spoil every chance I get. Molly was the gift that was happening for me, not what I thought was happening to me.

We all need to be patient enough to stop judgment so quickly on life issues and just see where things go. Perhaps what seems impossible or terribly unforgettable may just be the best thing that ever happened to you. Unless you free your mind and learn to control your inner game, you'll have an extremely hard time grasping this concept. If we could just step back from our primal reaction and be purposeful about our thought efforts and be disciplined in our thinking, perhaps we could see the forest through the trees.

The ability to control, or what I like to call free your mind, thoughts, and feeling towards a particular topic, is a crucial step in having the quality of life you deserve and being the most effective leader you can be. To be able to harness the energy which some try to take from you is a key element to success. Knowing what is worth fighting for and what is worth letting go is essential in your learning process and development as a true leader.

To get caught up in the day-to-day bull crap that sometimes goes on around you is certain suicide. Let the amateurs and, as Mark Cuban calls them, "Wantrepreneurs" deal with that. You ask, what's a "Wantrepreneur" and how do I know if I am one? Great question let me tell you what they are.

As my friend Marc Shuster would say it, "Wantrepreneurs are the 90-something percent of people who know they really want to do something but are missing the important ingredient of becoming a successful entrepreneur and the willingness to take action. Getting started is the vast majority of what creates the people who end up building the business for the people who don't. So there is never a perfect time to start. You will always think that you're earning a lot at work, you have other activities, you may have other costs in your life. But starting is the surest way to figure whether or not you have what it takes to be a real entrepreneur."

People claim that they are an Entrepreneur but in fact are actually are "wantrepeneurs." These days, there are many people who don't want to climb that corporate ladder or work for those corporate companies. They would prefer to be their own boss and take control of their own professional lives by building their own business or empire. Yet, there are big differences between being an entrepreneur and a "wantrepreneur", meaning you want that entrepreneurial life but don't execute it or pull it off.

- **Entrepreneurs: driven by their passion. "Wantrepreneurs": are interested in someone else's passion.**
You cannot force yourself to be passionate about something if you don't love it. You don't choose your passions, they choose you. An entrepreneur becomes successful because they do what it is they love and love

what it is they do. "Wantrepreneurs", on the other hand see what is proven successful by others and think that is what they need rather than want.

- **Entrepreneurs are innovators. "Wantrepreneurs" are procrastinators.**
Entrepreneurs understand that an idea doesn't have to be unique, different or original to allow it to be successful. They don't sit on their asses, waiting for the light bulb switch to turn on. Most times, the ultimate ideas come from seeing that what already exists needs improvement or that where a gap is, it needs to be filled. Most entrepreneurs, when starting their business venture to do so much research, looking for something they could not find anywhere else.

A "wantrepreneur" tends to obsessed about coming up with the perfect idea or what they think is the next big thing that will make them millions quickly.

- **Entrepreneurs accept failure and move on. "Wantrepreneurs" are prone to defeat.**
"I'm convinced that about half of what separates the successful entrepreneurs from the non-successful ones is pure perseverance."

– Steve Jobs.

All successful entrepreneurs will at some point meet failure. But they don't give up. They carry on and most times are more determined. It's where you will realize what's real from what's unreal. Doesn't matter how much time, money and effort was invested. Learning from your failures will help you to reach success later on. Trial & error is key to the entrepreneurial growth to success.

A "wantrepreneur," once they meet failure, will be defeated, discouraged and quit all together.

- **Entrepreneurs strive to be the best and "wantrepreneurs" just want to be rich.**
"Money is the trophy you get from doing the job well."

– Freeway Rick Ross

Entrepreneurs aim to be someone who helps leaders become leaders. They become role models and want to be the best within their industry. They do it for the love of their passion and to them, money is just a bonus. It is seen as a reward for doing great things. Entrepreneurs want to leave their mark in this world to encourage and inspire others to live their dreams. They believe in their passion before making profits.

"Wantrepreneurs" just care about themselves and the money. Entering your goals with money on your mind often leads to failure

- **Entrepreneurs work hard to achieve what they want. "Wantrepreneurs," wait for most things to be handed to them.**
Entrepreneurs work hard to get additional funds for their aspirations. They look for ways to raise capital for their business ventures. They do not wait to receive funding just to start. "Wantrepreneurs," on the other hand will sit and do absolutely nothing unless they receive the funds or capital they think they need to get a business rolling.

- **Entrepreneurs care about their business. "Wantrepreneurs" care about their image.**
Entrepreneurs are always too busy to worry about what the people around them are thinking about them.

"Wantrepreneurs" look for shortcuts. They have no patience to work hard building their business. They waste time creating an image of a successful business for others to believe in when in all actuality, they don't have anything done.

- **Entrepreneurs are lifetime students. "Wantrepreneurs" work based on the few courses they took.**
"My biggest motivation? Just to keep challenging myself. I see life almost like one long University education that I never had — everyday I'm learning something new." —

Richard Branson

Entrepreneurs love to learn everyday. They love challenges. Not necessarily learning in a classroom. They learn by getting out there in the real world. Learning from their failures. Learning from their mentors, even learning from those they inspire or by sitting in a cafe over good conversation. They are passionate about learning as they are about their business. Their minds are always open.

"Wantrepreneurs" think that taking a few classes and reading a textbook or two is all they need to succeed. They are more closed minded and don't think outside of the box. Not to say it's not good to be book smart, but it also pays to be street smart.

- **Entrepreneurs take risks to be successful. "Wantrepreneurs" want the success now.**
Entrepreneurs give it their all. They live by the thought of "I have nothing to lose but everything to gain". They know that the world of business is tough and competitive and that only a small percentage survive this shark filled tank. They risk their financial livelihood, their circle of friends, their image and even their own business and they aren't afraid of losing it because they believe so much in their product, service or business. They understand that there are risks involved to become successful. Living the entrepreneurial lifestyle comes with sacrifice. While

entrepreneurs would love to have a nice steak dinner all the time, they don't mind living off a can of sardines or instant noodle soup. They know all this, yet they put out. Pushing your ideas doesn't mean you have to look the part. It means you have to work harder and smarter to reach your goals.

"Wantrepreneurs" are mostly talk, no action. They back out when they feel they need to lose something to gain something. They just want to go in with a sure bet to success.

- **Entrepreneurs execute. "Wantrepreneurs" make excuses.**

Pessimism would be the arch nemesis of an entrepreneur, if an entrepreneur would be a super-hero. Being an entrepreneur is about following through. Going beyond your limits with determination and coming face to face with failure but never backing down.

"Wantrepreneurs" are like sore losers. They make excuses like, "I don't have time, I'm too busy with other things." Or, "I don't have enough money." They want to be their own boss but they're stuck in the employee mentality. They make excuses not to even try. They complain when it starts to get hard and quit.

- **Entrepreneurs believe that their team is everything. "Wantrepreneurs" think the business is about them.**

Not only does an entrepreneur believe in themselves, they believe in their team. They understand that their team is what helps the business succeed. They know they can't do it all on their own. They know the value of leadership and teamwork. Entrepreneurs know that their team is essential to the growth of the business to succeed. A great idea starts with the right leader and with the right people to organize and work together in all ways possible.

- **Entrepreneurs adapt. "Wantrepreneurs" call meetings.**

When things change in the environment of the business, an entrepreneur will adapt quickly and would find opportunities with the changes. Whether it's tapping into another market or a better and more refreshing way of initiating things.

"Wantrepreneurs" are likely to be left behind because they are too busy discussing every single aspect of the change. They are shaken by change. They hate change. They only want what they're used to doing.

As I hope you're starting to see, it is all in your head. There is nothing overly complicated about what it is I'm writing about. To free your mind is to think clearly about an objective, see it objectively, and go execute to the fullest of your capabilities. The limiting stories that you put on yourself is nothing but a mere strangle hold on your life, your business, your bank account and ultimately, your future. Change the old limiting beliefs you have and start living the life you were meant to have. No one's going to do it for you, if they were, it would have been done by now. You know what you need to do, it all starts with a plan of action, a little momentum and massive action until you get what you've earned. I do mean, what you've earned. We don't always get what we want, but we get you we've earned. Time to start putting in the work now. Your future self with thank you.

I've found one constant in my work and coaching and it seems to be true across the board and is no different if you're a doctor, lawyer, professional athlete, stay at home parent, small business owner or an eccentric billionaire. We will all do more for the people that we love than we will for ourselves. So why do I write this? I write this because we are wired to help, be giving, take care of the ones we love. So perhaps if you need some motivation to start, go announce what you're going to do, whatever it might be, to someone who loves you and best of all who will hold you accountable.

I have a perfect example for my situation and writing this book. My son, Gavin Michael Zamucen just turned six years old this past June and he knows quite well that I'm writing my third book. He likes to ask me what it's about and if it will have any pictures in it, specifically pictures of dinosaurs or great white sharks. I just laugh and tell him no, it's not that kind of book so he asks when will it be finished so he can take a look. I assume he wants to confirm that there really are no dinosaurs or great white sharks in the book. Everyday he asks if I stayed up late to write and if I'm finished. Gavin holds me accountable for this book, even if he doesn't know he's doing so. He is my "why" for staying up late, outlining chapters, writing deleting and re-writing sections so that they reflect my true meanings. I do it for him so he can see the pages and confirm, "Yep, no dinosaurs or great white sharks."

To be able to push yourself from something greater then yourself, just might be the motivation you need. Again, we tend to do more for others then we do for ourselves, don't you find this to be true for your own life?

Free your mind and do what you were put on this earth to do. Live the life you were meant to live. Share the gifts your Creator has given you. Be the person you were meant to be and never apologies for your greatness.

You Hold the Key.

I Hate Losing More Then I Like Winning

"You get on base, we win. You don't, we lose. And I hate losing. I hate it! I hate losing more than I even wanna win."

-Billy Beane General Manager, Oakland Athletics

Different people interpret this quote in distinctive ways. Some look at it as a super competitive man hating to lose so much he has a deeper visceral reaction to it than even winning. I have heard people say this quote was the most un-sportsmanlike quote they have ever heard. Of course, I understand their opinions and respect where they're coming from, but I do not see the quote the same way. To be perfectly clear, I agree with this quote one hundred percent, but perhaps from a different view.

I expect to win at everything I do. I do not care if it is a pickup basketball game, a board game, video game or business venture, bottom line, I expect to win. This is why I hate to lose more then I like winning, it is due in part to expectations of mine. Why would one think differently? For the love of the game? Maybe, but why be competitive in life just to get by. A 50/50 record is a failure in my book. I don't go through life to just play the game, I am here to win and win big.

There is some serious upside in life in being this way. In turn, there is some downside to being this way too. I will address them both, but I believe there is much more upside then downside. The downside is purely a mindset and as I write that, the upside is too. But, let's not get too wrapped up in the details before I explain what I mean.

When you expect to win in every aspect of life, you tend to win a lot, or at least a more measurable amount than not winning. If you start anything with purpose rather then just "doing", you seem to have a greater outcome for what you want and usually I like to win, so I do. Let me explain more of what I mean. You might want to grab a highlighter now, because I am about to give you some simple, yet extremely effective tools for getting what you want, or in other words, ways to win.

Let us think of something simple, what about having a great day with your kids. If you wanted to do that, how would you? You would probably plan the day, have certain events you may want to do at specific times and when it all begins and when it all ends. You are off to a great start, but to make sure you win at this day you may be missing a key ingredient. The missing ingredient is having an outcome for the day. If the day is just to have fun and to be more connected with your kids then you have to plan that into your day. You need to be very clear on the outcome of the day, a goal if you will. A goal is just a wish with a timeline, so make it for today. You need to plan on having a great day, but the key to having even more meaning to the day is to minimize or even better extinguish your expectations for the day. Have no expectations and appreciate every moment because some people would kill to be with the kids for just one more day. Appreciate the little things, the funny comments, the childlike behavior and get down with them and play a little. Get a little crazy and silly, just try being at their level for a few hours. It might just turnout to be one of the most rewarding days of your life. It is not the events in your life that really shape your existence, it is how you respond to those events. How you practice winning in every situation. Winning is a habit just like greatness is a habit. Practice the art of winning, greatness and overall fulfillment and in time you wont have to practice, it'll just be you.

If I am going to a meeting, it doesn't matter with whom it is with, I have an outcome I'm looking for. I never go into a meeting without a winning outcome. I always have an agenda in my head for what I want out of a situation, even if it is to have a good time. Plan on excellence and excellence will follow. Life will give you what you ask of it and usually more if you are extremely detailed when you ask. Again, life will give of you what you ask of it, so do not sell yourself short. If you are going to dream and shoot for the stars, then go for the biggest and brightest one because if you don't hit it at least you came much further than anyone expected. Life becomes pretty great when you plan to win.

The downside to this principle, if there is one, to "hate losing more than liking to win", I expect to win so in those rare moments of losing, I'm a terrible sore loser. When you expect to win and you do not, it hits you like a ton of bricks. It is a big slap in the face and at times hard to deal with. I personally find myself obsessing over a loss and doing tons of homework to be better prepared for the next round because I hate the feeling of losing. I must admit, it can be something as simple as a board game (and my wife can attest to this statement!) I have found myself laying in bed playing back in my head every move that was made to try to figure the key moment of the loss. If a loss is tracked you can normally find the exact move that caused the loss.

"Winning isn't everything, it's the only thing. Show me a good loser and I'll show you a loser."

-Vince Lombardi

One of my downfalls is taking the caption above to heart. I am not a good loser in any stretch of the imagination. If you are OK losing then you are probably used to it. Well, I am not used to it and I hate it. I hate losing with a passion and I get upset with people who are OK with losing. I remember being on teams in my life and losing a game or losing a client and having someone on the team say, "well, we gave it a good go". We gave it a good go? "Well I guess we should just go have a beer and celebrate being a loser." Not me, you will never see me celebrating mediocrity and in my opinion neither should you.

Let's face it, we live in a society where winning gets the spoils and losing just gets told to take a walk. This life of ours, this gift that you have been given by your Creator, this human experience only comes around once from

what I know. I want to make the most of it. I want to
expect more from myself, more out of this life, more than
people expect because why the hell not? Someone is
going to be rich, someone is going to drive that Ferrari,
someone is going to own that Rolls Royce, some is going
to buy that jet, someone is going to live your dream if
you let them. Do not let them, you deserve your dreams,
do you not? Why should you look at the car next to you
wishing you were driving that car instead of what you are
driving? Driving through neighborhoods thinking how
nice it would be to live in that "perfect" house? How nice
it would be to send your kids to that private school where
they learn Latin beginning in second grade because it is
the root of all language, and therefore they will be able to
easier learn and speak many different languages.

You want all of this? Good, start winning and start
winning everyday. Stop being complacent with your life
and expecting things to change. The road to "someday"
lead's to the land of never and "woulda, coulda,
shoulda"! Do not settle for OK, being OK sucks. Being
just OK does not lead to a life of fulfillment. Develop a
hatred of losing. You should become sick to your
stomach to think someone is better then you, something
is out of your reach, or something cannot be
accomplished. Stop telling yourself bullshit stories of
why you can't do this or that because that just leads you
to unhappiness and a life of regret. Do not be that person

at 85 that is telling people to not waste their life like you did and saying if you only had it to do over again.

"Your time is limited, so don't waste it living someone else's life."

-Steve Jobs

This is your wake up call and today, tonight, right now is the beginning of the rest of your life. The design of your life starts here. Now let me share with you some tools. Some of what I share with you I have picked up throughout the years from my personal coaches. Some of these tools were picked from Tony Robbins, Jim Rohn, Jordan Belfort, and some are my own. I would highly encourage you to follow and study the gentlemen in the previous sentence. They are all experts in their field and can certainly help most anyone with their work.

I live my life to maintain my own happiness while trying my best to not cause unhappiness to anyone else. If you want to be happy you need to understand that you can be happy and that you deserve to be happy and to win at this game of life. Many people make the mistake of believing that they don't deserve happiness and accept their unhappy state as their destiny, this is complete nonsense and a destructive thought. The truth of the matter is that happiness, like anything else in life, needs to be nurtured, massaged and executed on. The following are a few tips to create happiness in life and a winning state.

- Understand what it is that will make you happy. Everyone has unique requirements for attaining happiness and what makes one person happy may be very different from what makes someone else happy. Rejoice in your individuality and do not worry about whether or not your desires are comparable to those of your peers. You are living life for you and if you are not fully happy and fulfilled in life, you are not winning.

- Make a plan for attaining goals and make a plan to win. Your mood will likely increase as your pursue your goal because you will feel better about yourself for going after something you value. Let's face it, winning feels better then losing.

- Surround yourself with good people. It is easy to begin to think negatively when you are surrounded by people who think that way. Conversely, if you are around people who are happy their emotional state will be infectious. Have you ever started laughing or at minimum started smiling because you heard someone laugh. It is biochemistry, it happens to all of us. Ever laugh in a movie theater at things you would never laugh at when you were alone at home? Of course, we all do. Laughter, playfulness, fun, it is all contagious energy. If you still are not convinced, go visit a kindergarten class and just say the word "booger". Take note of their reaction, I smile just thinking about their little faces.

- When something goes wrong try to figure out a solution instead of wallowing in self pity. Truly happy people don't allow setbacks to affect their mood because they know that with a little thought they can turn the circumstances back to their favor. That is a secret spice to winning. The goal is not to have a problem free life, because problems and failures are how we grow and learn. It is not if you fail, you will, many times over, but you need to learn to fail correctly. No one cares about you failing as much as you do. So sitting around and feeling sorry for yourself does little for your life. Reflection on a situation is fine, wallowing in self-pity is a loser emotion that you should not let yourself get away with.

- Spend a few minutes each day thinking about the things that make you happy. These few minutes will give you the opportunity to focus on the positive things in your life and will lead you to continued happiness. I learned from Tony Robbins about what he calls "priming" in the morning before I start my day. I spend ten to twenty minutes each morning getting myself in that state of gratefulness. I ask myself, "Who am I grateful for? What am I grateful for? Why am I grateful for these things? How does that make me feel?" I really get in the moment and feel those feelings. It is a great way to start the day.

- It's also important to take some time each day to do something nice for yourself. Whether you treat yourself to lunch, take a long, relaxing bath or simply spend a few extra minutes on your appearance you will be subconsciously putting yourself in a better mood. If you are constantly giving to others and not yourself you'll crap out. You need balance in your life, no need to be extreme at everything, with the exception of winning, always win.

- Finding the humor in situations can also lead to happiness. While there are times that require you to be serious, when it is appropriate, find a way to make light of a situation that would otherwise make you unhappy. If you say to yourself or someone else, we will laugh about this in a year, than why not laugh now. Why suffer for the year? Laugh now, what is done is done so perhaps from laughing you will get yourself a better state of mind and figure out how whatever happened will not ever happen again.

- Maintaining your health is another way to achieve happiness. Being overweight or not eating nutritious foods can have a negative effect on your mood. Additionally, exercise has been known to release endorphins that give you a feeling of happiness. Motion creates emotion. Get off your ass and get moving. It is hard to be depressed about life when you are dancing through it. Just get moving.

- Finally, it is important to understand that you deserve happiness. Those who believe that they are not worthy of happiness may subconsciously sabotage their efforts to achieve happiness. Don't be that person, don't run the pattern of failure. You are better than that and if you don't think you are, put this damn book down or go give it to someone who will read it and improve their life.

You will lose, we will all fail from time to time, we will all crash massively but it is not a bad thing to do so. You learn many lessons from a loss. The important thing is that you know how to handle failure. Failure just might be the fire you need for greatness. I expect you to win and in turn I also expect you to learn from setbacks so failure becomes a state of mind in which you control. Control failure, do not let it control you.

"You build on failure. You use it as a stepping-stone. Close the door on the past. You don't try to forget the mistakes, but you don't dwell on it. You don't let it have any of your energy, or any of your time, or any of your space."

- Johnny Cash

You Hold the Key.

No, Screw You

"Are you not ashamed of caring so much for the making of money and for fame and prestige, when you neither think nor care about wisdom and truth and the improvement of your soul?"

-Socrates

To write on a subject that is so personal to some and certainly to me means I must write the truth. Not what some people want to believe is the truth, but the hard honest truth. People will, at some point in your career, try to screw you in one way or another. This is just a simple fact of life. Again, lets face it, there are some people in the world who are just assholes. There is nothing you can do about it. It is hard to always avoid these people, because at times these people will be your best friends or possibly family members. Not all the ghouls in your life will be hiding in the shadows, a lot of time you invite them to the dinner table.

Let me take you on two personal journeys of people screwing me in my business life. The first story is one of pure greed, backhandedness, deception, stealing and cheating. The second story is one of nothing but complete disappointment. Nonetheless, both of these stories I got screwed in and there was nothing I could have done about it.

Cautionary tale one:

In one of my successful operations I began to franchise my company, where as someone would pay my company a fee for our logo, marketing plans, extensive training, ongoing support and in return they pay a royalty from their sales. Franchising can truly be a winning situation for both parties if done correctly. I happen to be good at showing people how to become successful entrepreneurs, so good, in fact, it turned a few greedy. Let me explain.

We have a company which is a well-known national brand and it is in a very unique niche space. Our company dominates in almost every major market in the country outside of a few select cities we intentionally stay out of for various reasons. Our systems are so dominating in our niche space and we have trained people so well, our franchises lives have been financially propelled from middle income when they started to excellent six figure careers from investing into my franchise. To be fair, some even seven figures within the first two years of franchise ownership. I am very proud of that, to be able to change someone's life for the better because they made the right decision for themselves and bought my franchise. It is really something that makes me feel great about capitalism. Unfortunately, there is another side of the coin, the greed side of business.

The greed comes into business when one party does not want to pay their fair agreed upon share, which in franchising we call royalties. Franchisees pay royalties for national marketing events, support, legal issues, job creation, etc. There are many things the franchisor does to help the franchisees. The problem is some franchisees want to be, or feel special. They want to standout from the crowd and have rules bent or eliminated just for them, because they are such special creatures. A creature is stating it nicely.

A few of those creatures did not want to pay royalties

anymore. They felt they had outgrown the franchise system and did not need us anymore. They felt they could do it on their own with no further support from corporate. While this may have been true in some aspects, such as having enough contacts locally to support their business, knowing where to buy products and not having a need anymore for franchise marketing support, there was one big problem in front of these few bottom feeders. They willingly signed franchises agreements binding them to their word. Now, for most people in the western civilized world, when you sign a legal contract you abide by that contract. You abide by that contract even when you want out, you wait out the contract you signed and then don't re-sign another one. Nonetheless, bottom feeders just do not think this way. Bottom feeders are always looking for an angle to screw someone and as I've said before in this book, if you look hard enough you'll always find a way. This is true even if you are looking to be a dishonest piece of crap.

So to get out of a legally binding contract what do you do? You go get a shady attorney who is just looking to screw the big bad franchisor and help their piece of crap clients gain "justice." How these types of attorneys sleep at night I have no idea. I think they like screwing people for a living personally. These two franchises grab the biggest, loudest, greasiest attorney they could find who would exploit any weakness in the agreement. Let me give you a little tip, the reason why no one likes attorneys is because they get paid to disrupt the course of business. They drool over this kind of work. Nothing but "telephone tough guys," as I call them.

Quick back story on both of these franchises who wanted out of the system so badly. One was making over a million dollars a year with us and the other was making over three quarters of a million dollars a year. Prior to being a part of my franchise system, the most they ever made in their life time was less than a hundred thousand a year. That's right, we took them from their miserable corporate life to making a million dollars a year, following our systems, our game plan, our blue print. A few years in though, once they had tasted success at a level they had never known before, they wanted out and felt they did not need the system anymore. Rather than thanking us for changing their life for the better and showing them how to really make great money, their greed stepped in and now they wanted out. They not only wanted out but they were preparing to sue me for $1.7 million dollars each. They wanted to sue for $3.4 million dollars because of a missing line item. Greed is always lurking in the wings.

These were two guys that begged me to let them into the system. I must admit, I had major reservations with letting either one of them in and now I know why, because they were, and are pieces of shit who are just assholes I cannot help because I have done enough. In the beginning of their franchises, it was thank you so much for letting me in, you've changed my life and then it was the same old same, "what have you done for me lately?" They began to gripe about the royalties, then a few months later it was about our products, then it was how we are not advertising enough for them and not driving business to them. Again, they were making respectively a million dollars a year. I think we did a pretty good job, so good, they must have gotten confused on why they were making the kind of money they only dreamt about before joining us. They were making the money because of us, not in lieu of us. Greed kind of blinds a person.

So with their ridiculous attorney's help, of course they felt they found a loophole in the franchise agreement. One little line out of 56 pages that they were going to hold onto like a pit-bull on a bloodied rope swinging on the old oak tree in back. When they brought it to our legal counsel they had their proverbial chests puffed out thinking they had us now and we were going to just fold and let them walk. Nope, not the case with us. What they found was pretty immaterial, but enough to stir some rumors amongst the rest of the peaceful happy franchises. These creatures went on a mission to call every operational franchise and some non-operational because they left the system or sold and told them we had to give back their franchise fee because they "discovered" an omission on our agreement. Yes, their entire platform was based on finding an omission we simply failed to mention because we did not know we were required to per federal regulations. So they found a one-line mistake and tried to infect the entire company so we would let them out of their agreements. We, in fact, did let them out of their agreements and to be fair to the others in the system we offered back everyone's franchise fees. We said anyone who wanted out of the system because of our mistake, we would be let out with no questions asked, and even give them back the franchise fee they paid (which was around forty thousand dollars per location.) We even went as far as to offer this to people who were no longer with the franchise. Why would we do this? Simple, you always do what is right, or else the wrong you have done will come back at you. Karma is a bitch and these creatures that started this will get what is coming to them, I can guarantee that.

To finish with this story, we paid out about a million dollars when all said and done. About twelve franchises left the system, though only five were active, so there was really no harm done. I know that a million dollars sounds like a lot of money to lose, and it is. Yet, when you have a strong business, an even stronger management and legal team, and excellent advisors around you, you can handle almost anything. We did not miss a beat, the business today is bigger and stronger then ever and still continues to grow. What happened to the former franchises that started this? They received nothing, absolutely nothing. They received a lot of legal bills and absolutely no money. They did leave the system, but they got kicked out like the dogs they are. Greed overshadows rational thought. Be careful who you let into your system, your company, and your life.

The second story is one of disappointment and frankly it is a lot shorter tale. I have a friend whom I loaned a substantial amount of money to for him to open a business. I paid for the business, we had a contract of how he and his partner would pay me back and it worked for about four months. Well, they had a 60-month payment plan and after four months they terminated their business relationship and 20 year friendship and split up. The company survived as my buddy bought his partner out and things seemed to be going as planned. A month went by after the breakup and no payment to me, two months, four months, six months, eight months…do you see a pattern here?

My buddy and I had an agreement about how the business was to be paid back and even in the breakup with his partner, my buddy took over all company debt because he took the business. Well, it was, and still to this day the biggest debt he has and he has paid me once over the last year. The question is what to do about it when your friend is not intentionally screwing you, but nevertheless is still in fact screwing you. I would imagine my buddy feels that the reason he does not need to pay me is because I must understand that things are tight for him and frankly, I do not need the money. While I certainly understand this thought process, the part that makes me mad is that I am guessing this is what he is thinking. He basically avoids me and has little communication with me unless he needs advice on the business I funded. When I do bring it up I hear nothing but, "there's just major money problems" and "a lot of money stress going on." Again, I understand the avoidance, I don't justify it, because I would not do that, but I guess there is a sense of insecurity and shame with him.

I've been pretty fair about this. I cut his payments, I cut the interest on the loan, I have offered him ways out, I even said to him, "I do not care what you pay me, just pay me something every month so I know you haven't forgotten about this" and still, nothing. See, you will have to make a decision at some point in your life of what is the most important things to you. This is a time where I have chosen my friendship with my buddy over the money.

People will screw you and that's just part of life. It's not what happens to you in life, it's the decisions you make about what happens to you, which shapes your life. The key is to play the hand you were dealt as if that was the exact had you wanted. It is our decisions that shape us, not our environment. You have complete control of your life. Start exercising it.

If you hear a voice within you say "you cannot paint," then by all means paint and that voice will be silenced.

-Vincent Van Gogh

You Hold the Key.

This next small section below was added three weeks after I finished previous section above:

While buying a new home I encountered a seller who had a home for sale my wife liked very much. I was fine with it as I had my favorite, but those of you who are married you know "Happy Wife...", so we went with her number one pick.

I submitted my offer for the residence and it was accepted. We went under contract and the normal process started from there. We went through two appraisals, two because of the price of the home, an inspection and all the normal underwriting paperwork etc. As normal in high-priced homes, we asked for an extension on time to close by a few days and the seller said no. The sellers would not budge, they said they would only consider an extension if we added $15,000 to contract.

Well, as a businessman when someone puts me in a no win crappy deal, I walk, and I did. I walked away from the house within my contractual agreed time to ensure I did not lose my earnest money of $100,000. I followed the complete terms of the contract and made sure everyone was aware I was bowing out. This is all in accordance with the agreement so no one was surprised or left holding the bag. When you exit an agreement you do so as you agreed upon in the beginning.

Apparently this did not sit well with the seller of the home. He felt the need to go on to the internet and bash one of my companies to somehow financially hurt me. Even though I did everything legally and per the mutual agreed upon contract, he must have felt wronged somehow. So, to get back at me was to attack one of my companies. Silly if you ask me, because there are always consequences when you try to harm someone else.

As I wrote in the previous section above, people will always try to screw you in one form or another. You don't have to like what is going on nor what people are doing, you simply have to deal with it. Keep a cool head and do not let your mind become jaded with revenge plans. To be clear I'm not saying just lay down and take it. If someone is attacking you, make sure it is the last time they ever think about doing it again. People need to understand your kindness is not a weakness, your kindness is just holding back the shark that lurks inside until it is time to strike. A shark never sleeps and needs to constantly eat. Time always runs out for all prey and the shark will pay an unforgettable vicious visit. Make no mistake, the shark is patiently planning, hunting and will strike when the time is right. Believe that.

Shark

Does a shark complain about Monday? NO! They are up early, biting stuff, chasing things, and creating fear for the others in the water, fish or man. They remind everyone at every moment of every day, that they're a shark and they don't apologize for being one. In fact, they love it.

-Author unknown expanded by Nick-Anthony Zamucen

I often wonder when I hear someone say, "Man it's already Monday tomorrow? Or I can't wait for the weekend!" And they say it every week. Why are they doing what they do on a daily basis? Why have they put themselves into being in a "working drone" mentality? If you do not like what you are doing, change. Yes, it really is that simple. Or do you not want your dreams enough to sacrifice your mediocre life? Are your dreams just that, a dream? Why could you not have it? Why are your dreams so scary to you? Are you more worried about what "if" you actually had them? Does it scare you?

To believe that people are actually more scared of success than failure has always been a head scratcher to me. It is a real thing and I see it literally everyday. People will lie to themselves and say they are not scared of the success, but I don't buy it. People either do not have big enough dreams, or they do not have enough pain to move towards their dreams. It is really one or the other.

Most people do not attack their dreams like a shark attacks its prey because they have not created enough internal pressure to do so. They have blinded themselves into believing their life is not that bad or most people don't achieve their dreams so they're not going to try. What if you fail? What if you put all this hard work in and you do not make it? "My God what if the sun blows up tomorrow and we all die?" Well, if that happens it does not matter anyhow, we are all dead. I suggest you change your thinking to what if it did happen? How would that change your life and the lives of those around you?

Lets be real for a moment shall we? For your dreams
to come true and for you to be financially free there is
a lot of work to do and it is not easy. Let me ask you,
is it easy every Monday morning to get out of bed and
get ready for that dead-end job? Is it easy to jump in
your "OK" car and sit in traffic to go to a job you do
not really like or the job you have convinced yourself
was "OK"? Is it easy to be told how much your worth
and that is all you'll make? Is it easy to have to ask for
vacation days off, like you had to ask your parents to
borrow the car when you were a teenager? Do you
like having to ask if you can live your life outside
your job? Is it easy to have to call in to work because
you need the day off and hope you can get that day
paid for because you have made the greatest sacrifice,
time for money? Does it make you feel safe and
secure knowing that one down turn in the company
can cost you your job and you can be let go because
of nothing you did wrong? Is it easy knowing
someone else is control of your future, good or bad?
Let me ask you this...how the hell do you sleep at
night? This illusion of security you have created for
yourself is just that, an illusion. Wake up! Take
control of your life and be willing to put in the effort
into becoming the person you were meant to be,
perhaps not the person you have turned into. You owe
you, so stop the bullshit you tell yourself and lets start

creating the life you deserve. Time to be a shark.

Here is another little fun fact for you, you do not need anyone's permission to go after your dreams. You do not need anyone's permission to strive for greatness. You do not need anyone's permission to go kick ass, you simply just make up your mind to do so and do it. Prove to those around you that whatever your "thing" is, is real, you can make it happen and this is exactly how it should be. No one needs to know the ins and outs of it all. No one should judge you for being the better you, although let me warn you, they will. Do not fool yourself success has many enemies. People will always try to tear you down during the process and then ask you how you did it when it is going great. There will always be naysayers and "Debbi Downers." Who cares? Who cares what those Monday morning armchair quarterbacks think. They will point the finger at your losses and award your success to "luck". Who cares about those fools who don't have the courage try go for it. Frankly, their opinion of you is none of your business anyways. Be a damn shark, scare the hell out of those clown fish with success.

Other people's opinions are cheap. Asking someone else what you should do with your life won't cost you much. Everyone around you will happily tell you their opinions on how you should live. "Don't be so selfish." "Give more to others." "Put other people first." People are happy to spew this kind of generalized nonsense at you all day long. All the opinions in the world can't override that persistent tug inside of you. Your inner voice, your instincts, your gut—it knows what's best for you. You know what's best for you.

The problem is that you've been taught to ask for other people's advice your entire life. You've been taught to value other people's gut reactions over your own instincts. It's time to start listening to yourself again. It's time to start relying on yourself. When you trust your instincts about yourself, you come out on top. When you bet on yourself, you win. Always.

Here are 5 strategies for you:

1. Ignore compliments but seek criticism.

Growth is a prime human need. If you're healthy, you'll always want to improve at something in your life. Your instincts should always tell you that there's more to learn. That you could be doing an even better job. This is why it's important to surround yourself with the right kind of people. Getting feedback from others is critical to growing quickly. But it has to be the right kind of feedback. Unsolicited opinions and compliments are useless.

Constructive criticism, on the other hand, is invaluable. The more painful, the better. The question is: can you handle the criticism? Can you love the criticism so much that you ask for it? Can you differentiate constructive criticism from useless compliments and ignore the latter? Look, even your most successful idol can blow you off just by giving you worthless feedback like "good job." Compliments like "good job" come from two different types of people. Those who feel threatened by what you're doing and want to hold you down, and those who haven't got a clue of what you're doing and wouldn't recognize if you did a good job or not. Either way, these kinds of compliments are meant to pacify you. At no point is your work done so well that you can't do better. There is always room for improvement. You always need to improve. You need real criticism. When someone provides you with constructive criticism, even if it's scathing, they're providing you with an opportunity to grow. The right kind of criticism will snap you to attention and help you grow.

The wrong kind will drag you down and demotivate you. It's up to you to be able to tell the difference. It's up to you to know who is really for you and who is against you. If you want to improve rapidly in life, start seeking constructive criticism and shying away from empty compliments.

2. Fight against popular opinions.

Your instinct is an incredible ability. It's inherent to you. It's a big reason why you've made it this far in life. It's one of your best resources for thriving as a human being. But you've been trained to ignore it. You've been trained to obey society's herd mentality and go along with what everyone else says is best for you. Popular opinions are usually wrong. You'll never be successful in life by following a consensus blueprint for what you *should* do. Go to college, graduate, get married, have 2.5 kids, work a mediocre job with a mediocre wage. Be safe. Be boring. Stay average. Tiptoe to the grave. If you listen to popular opinions like these, you deserve to be a nobody in life. You deserve to be dependent on other people for happiness and success. You don't need popular opinion to tell you what to do with your life, how to live it, or how to solve your problems. You know what you were meant to do with your life better than anyone else. Trust yourself. Bet on yourself. It's not a popular opinion to take bold, risky steps towards improving your life. It's not a popular opinion to eliminate the manipulative and toxic people from your life. Do it anyway. If you want to meet your goals, follow your gut and your rational mind, not society's impractical ideas about what's best for you.

3. Use unfamiliar situations as challenges.

Training your instinct is like training your body. Your mind is a muscle and it gets weak without use. If you want to become more mentally tough and independent in life, you need to start deliberately putting yourself in uncomfortable situations. You need to start putting yourself in adventurous situations. Stop being afraid of conflict. Stop shying away from failure. Instead, look for opportunities to fail and fail big. The bigger the opportunity to fail, the bigger the opportunity to succeed. The bigger the opportunity to win big and shock the world. When was the last time you shocked anyone? When was the last time you made a decision that made both you and others uncomfortable? Was it months ago? Years ago? It's time to start shaking things up again. You only have one life, one chance to rattle the cage and make something big happen for yourself. Quit wasting it. Get comfortable with uncertainty. Get comfortable with being uncomfortable. Don't settle for unhappiness for another 10 years, 20 months, or even another 10 days. Choose uncertainty over unhappiness. Uncertainty leads to growth, but unhappiness leads to nothing but misery.

4. Never act as a crutch for someone else.

Your instinct is very valuable. This is especially true when it comes to determining who is for you and who is against you. Too many people let negative friends and negative family members stay in their lives for years even though their guts tell them to cut the cord. These people reject their instincts. They reject their rational reasons. Instead, they give in to guilt. They feel bad for someone and instead of truly helping them by walking away, they give them handouts and act as a crutch. They empower their negative behavior. They support their malfunction. When you allow someone to be dependent on you, you weaken them. You also weaken yourself. Dependency produces dependence. When you allow dependence in your life, one way or another, you become more dependent. Quit giving other people a free pass to be negative or to play the victim. Quit giving other people handouts just because it's easier than saying "no." Show some courage. Show some tough love. Start encouraging others to stand on their own, not rely on you for help. This will make both you and them more self-reliant and successful in life.

5. Celebrate your victories, but don't dwell on them.

Your life is meant to be challenging, like a battle. When you challenge yourself, even if you fall short of your goals, you don't really fail. You don't really fail because you've forced your brain to adapt to something new. But what happens when you win? What happens when you overcome the obstacles in front of you and do what you set out to do, conquering a goal others told you was unrealistic? Do you just move on to the next goal? Do you absorb yourself in the praise others give you? No, you internalize your own victory. You validate yourself. You celebrate within.

Appreciate what you've been able to do on your own. Accept those who celebrate you too. But don't dwell on external praise. When you allow others to validate you, you become complacent. You forget what you really want out of life. You forget the importance of depending on your own validation. You dull your instincts and lose sight of the big picture. Instead of letting your victory define you, leverage it to your advantage. Use it as an example of how you can achieve even bigger goals. Let your victories compound and they'll push you forward. Let victory become instinctual.

Keep sharpening and improving your instincts by submerging yourself in the unknown. Look at the world from different perspectives and get out of your comfort zone. The more your instinct improves, the more you'll be able to trust it. The more you develop and trust your instincts, the more you'll be able to accomplish in life. The world will become less intimidating because you'll know how to cope with the challenges you face and work things out on your own. Do this and you'll live a more confident and focused life.

Don't be fooled. We all have setbacks. We all have times when nothing seems to work and we seem to tread water. Having the right, positive mindset, surrounding yourself with encouraging people, keeping yourself inspired and always knowing your goals will keep you on the right road to major success.

Let me share with you a few shark businessman and stories you may not know. Perhaps it will provide you a bit of leverage and encouragement to know that others have went through harder times and prevailed.

Henry Frick

His name isn't as well known as his partner's (Andrew Carnegie), but Henry Frick was the second half of Carnegie Steel. Together they dominated the American steel industry in the 1800s.

Frick was infamous for his hatred of unions. Perhaps his most notorious act happened in 1892 during the

Homestead Strike, when the Carnegie steel union went on strike. Unwilling to give into the union's demands, Frick closed the mill and locked out 3,800 men. Two days later, workers seized the mill. Frick then hired a private police force to take the mill back. After 12 hours of fighting, ten people were dead, including three workers and three private police officers.

A few months after the famous strike, a union supporter snuck into Frick's office and shot him. Frick fell to the ground then stood back up and tackled the shooter. While fighting on the ground, Frick was stabbed four times. He was back at work a week later.

Robert Moses

You most likely have no idea who Robert Moses is, but you certainly know his work. A mostly anonymous but powerful figure in New York from around the mid-1900s, Moses is responsible for building Shea Stadium, Lincoln Center, Jones Beach, the United Nations headquarters in New York, the 1964 World's Fair, Jones Beach, the Henry Hudson Parkway, the Central Park Zoo, Bryant Park, the Triborough Bridge, and virtually every other major New York construction project.

While the magnitude of those accomplishments is tough to grasp, according to his biographer, at the height of his power Moses "had more power, more money, more tangible, physical property to his name than just about anyone…ever."

Although the words "city planner" and "badass" are rarely put together, Moses was a quiet, string-pulling bureaucrat in the background of New York City when he was the city planner from 1920 to 1950. So what exactly does that mean?

Moses single-handedly shaped New York City's layout. He was uneducated, untrained, rarely drove a car (even though he designed New York's highways), and didn't take a salary. During his time as city planner, Moses built 13 bridges, 416 miles of parkways, 658 playgrounds, and 150,000 housing units, which cost $150 billion in today's dollars and displaced 250,000 New Yorkers.

So why would such an ambitious man become a civil servant? Moses was driven by power. He often claimed that he wanted to build parks for a living, but his love of parks was really a front for his true goal: turning New York into his own empire.

One writer said of Moses, "The public couldn't stop him, the mayor couldn't stop him, the governor couldn't stop him, and only once could the President of the United States stop him." Moses was famous for always being on the go and rarely reflecting. He never asked why, he only did, which ultimately made him one of the most polarizing figures of the 1900s.

Samuel "Sam" Zemurray

Nicknamed "Sam the Banana Man," Samuel
Zemurray is the man behind the United Fruit
Company.

In 1909, after selling bananas in America for a few
years, Zemurray traveled to Honduras to buy a farm in
hopes of cutting out the middle man. After the
Honduran government protested his presence,
Zemurray hired an army he recruited in New Orleans
and overthrew the Honduran government. Soon, he
began buying shares in the United Fruit Company and
eventually took it over in 1932.

So just how big was Zemurray?

At one point, United Fruit Company owned 70% of
Guatemala, employed 100,000 people in a dozen
countries, and commanded the largest private navy in
the world. He was an oval office confidante of
Franklin Roosevelt and played a huge role in the
founding of Israel.

And yet this immigrant with the Russian accent
remained an outsider. He never broke into the upper
crust social world of New Orleans or Boston, where
his North American business interests were centered.

"For most people, even in New Orleans, Zemurray is
a forgotten man, but his life is an epic American
story," Zemurray's biographer said. A hands-on
manager, Zemurray often showed up in the fields and

on the New Orleans docks, seeking ideas from
employees.

David Ogilvy

David Ogilvy is one of the creators of modern-day
advertising. Before Ogilvy, marketers were reserved
and well-mannered. Ogilvy was the opposite. He is
famous for his flamboyant style, charm, decisive
thinking, and aggressiveness.

Ogilvy started his first ad agency in 1948. By this
time he had worked as a sous-chef, an advertising
trainee, a door-to-door salesman for the stove
company Aga, a researcher for George Gallup about
Americans' opinions on movie stars, an Amish-
country farm owner, and a spy for British military
intelligence during World War II.

After becoming the go-to salesman in his 20s, Ogilvy
wrote a book on sales. "The good salesman combines
the tenacity of a bulldog with the manners of a
spaniel," Ogilvy wrote. "If you have any charm, ooze
it."

In addition to being an advertising mastermind,
Ogilvy loved ostentatious clothing, private clubs, and
Rolls Royce's. Equally as famous as his work, Ogilvy
owned the 30-room Château de Touffou south of
France's Loire Valley, where he retired seven years
later with his third wife, a woman 25 years his junior.

According to Bloomberg, "from France, Ogilvy bombarded employees with up to 50 faxed memos per day, but his influence waned. So, too, did his vast wealth, owing to his profligate spending."

All of these men had reason to quit, call time-out, and rethink their game, but they all stayed in the game to become sharks.

"Things may come to those who wait, but only the things left by those who hustle."

-Abraham Lincoln

You Hold the Key.

In the Still of the Night

"Sleep, those little slices of death – how I loathe them."

-Attributed to Edger Allan Poe

From a child I have always had a hard time sleeping. I remember getting spanked because I would not fall asleep fast enough. Funny now as an adult with children of my own, spanking them because they would not fall asleep in a certain time frame seems a bit barbaric, but hey my childhood was not average in any sense. I've said it before, because of my childhood and my upbringing it helped shape who I am today. I would not change it for a "better" one because I know people who had great childhoods and loving mothers who baked them cookies and were the classroom mom who went on all the fieldtrips. They are usually the people that expect things to be done for them. They are the ones who sleep well at night. The ones I beat on an hourly, daily, and yearly measure.

See my ability to stay awake for literally days has helped me tremendously in my business career. No sleeping has given me an advantage over my "assumed" competition. I write "assumed" because my real competition is me. I am more demanding of myself then anyone could possibly be. I chase the future me knowing I will never catch him. It keeps me hungry and humble. Not taking the time for, what I call, excessive sleep has given me the edge I need to consistently win, stay on top, beat those around me. See, when they sleep, I work. When they eat or watch TV, I work. When they complain to their spouses about why their life is not what they want, I work. When they go have too many beers with their friends and try to numb their life, I work. Currently as I sit in front of my computer writing this chapter it is 2:17am on Monday night or you may say Tuesday morning.

Working through the night like a ghost allows me the ability to beat them every time. The simple reason is this, while they work from nine to five and take weekends off, the reality is they are not working nine to five. They might be at their office at nine, but they jack around for three to four hours of the day and only really accomplish about four hours of real work. That means they are only putting in about 20 hours of real work into their company per week. 20 hours, I do that in normally a day. My day is their week. Any questions of why I win? It is very simple math. I use about ten times more hours during the day being productive then they do. I simply out work them and have trained my body to handle this workload throughout the years. If you do the math, I do a full year's worth of work in about 53 calendar days. I do take Sundays off to be with my family, family is always first, so if you add back those days, I do an average year of work in about 61 calendar days. That is right and to scale it out further, I work an average of four years to the average persons year. To give you an example, it takes most people seven to nine months to create a 150-page book. I have two chapters left, and I have been working on this book for less than 40 days.

My advantage is not needing what some would call a full night's sleep. I hear all the time, "Nick not everyone is you, some of us need sleep you cyborg robot machine creature". While I find this humorous, I am here to tell you, sleep is overrated and can be overcome with practice and persistence. Your body is an amazing thing, the harder you push it the better it performs. This goes for working out and getting stronger. Using your mind and becoming a speed-reader. To working your way into sleeping less so you can become more productive.

Think of it like this. Your body while sleeping is basically in shutdown mode. Let's say you shutdown for the recommended seven to nine hours a night for sleep. You body is resting for seven plus hours, that is unbelievable to me. You must jump right out of bed and say, "I feel so rested and great after my hours and hours of sleep! I'm ready to take on the world!" I seriously doubt you do that. If you are like most people, you wake up slowly, not talking to too many people or as little as possible before you have your one to three cups of coffee. Then you get in the shower, stretching and yawning the whole way thinking how tired you are. Then maybe after the shower you start feeling like a normal human again. Does this sound familiar?

Let me ask you, why do you feel this way? I mean after all you just had nine hours of sleep, where your body was unconscious and immobile. It is not like you were running a marathon while you were sleeping all those hours. You were lying there, breathing slowly and deeply. In a totally relaxed unconscious state, correct? So why are you waking up tired? Perhaps because you have trained your mind and body differently then I have mine. I would venture to say that getting even more sleep is not the answer to you being tired. I would say you being tired throughout the day has very little with you being actually sleepy. I would say it has more to do with your conditioned laziness then actual sleep. You do not need more sleep, you need more of a reason to get up and get moving.

Want to know why you ask a busy person to get something done and not the one with not a lot to do? Simple, because the busy person is used to doing things so things will get done. A person who has nothing to do will take forever for a simple task, if it even gets done. Don't you find this to be true? Let me give you an example I would think we could all agree on. Ever go to a restaurant when it is not busy? Your food seems to take forever to come out after you order. The service is sub-par, the food comes out incorrect and the manger is nowhere to be found. Why is this? It is because when they are slow the restaurant is not in a rhythm of success. The waiter takes longer to put the order in, because he or she is talking to other wait staff or flirting with the underage hostess. The cooks are prepping for the next service and not looking at the tickets coming in as they do when they are busy, the manager is counting a drawer or checking side-work so he can downsize the staff in the slow time not thinking about who is walking in the door and the bar tender making drinks is leaning on the taps chatting with the regulars, who unfortunately you are not one of. See the whole place gets out of rhythm and the worst part is this happens everyday in almost every restaurant in America and this is why you have a certain restaurant in your head you are thinking about right now. They have conditioned themselves to fail from 2pm-5pm daily. Are you doing this with your business? Do you have a competitive advantage for your business and over your competition? I would assume you do, you just either 1. Are not using it to its full potential or 2. You do not in fact know what it is.

If you've ever Google searched your business's specific practice, you'll have discovered many businesses sound and look just like yours. That's the trouble with trying to get noticed in a crowded marketplace. Since he published Competitive Advantage in 2008, Harvard professor Michael Porter has been the undisputed authority of what it takes to stand out from the crowd. His theory on competitive advantage took some of the older theories like finding unique selling points and value propositions out of the hands of marketers and gave strategic responsibility for creating genuine competition to managers. Simply put, he says competitive advantage is the ability of a business to beat others on price or value.

Every business, even in a world of generic products and near-identical competitors needs to find its unique advantage. Nailing competitive advantage, Porter says, should always result in better or different value for the consumer and higher profitability for the business, a mutual win. Fail to nail and disaster can ensue. Take the example of American coffee giant Starbucks, who tried in vain to conquer the Australian coffee market. It opened its first store amidst a media blitz in 2000 but by August 2008 was forced to shut 61 of its 84 Australian cafes.

It was the same year, according to IbisWorld, that Australians spent $752 million on cups of retail coffee alone. So, where did Starbucks go wrong? At the heart of its failure was the US company's unwillingness to alter its offering to woo the coffee drinkers of Australia who already had an engrained coffee culture. In other words, it failed to provide better or different value to the coffee retailers already established around Australia.

The failure of another US import to Australia is Quizno Sub to capture some of the market share of the lucrative Subway brand was another example of absent competitive advantage. Apart from illegalities surrounding its franchising disclosures, Quizno was also blind to its Australian market, using entirely US-based menus and services. In fact, it's only real competitive edge was that it would first toast the sandwiches it filled. Subway's response? It introduced the option to you're your sandwich toasted and Quizno quickly fell.

But if the big brands get it wrong, how can small businesses hope to succeed?

Alchemy business consultant and accountant Roxanne Hoskinson says, "Look at your competitors as a starting point to see what your competitor is doing wrong that you can fix," she said. "Complaints are the best way to find out how to get things done properly. "Listen to your market and hear what they're whispering about your competitors."

Author Tom McKaskill agrees, saying thorough research on both competitors and consumers is essential to determining competitive advantage.

"Unless you want to exist in a stagnant state where... you face a future of slow death, you need to find some dimension in your product or service that has greater appeal to a segment of the market than your competitors," he says. He goes further to say the importance of continually creating and sustaining customer value has to be hardwired into every business plan. "Only by moving away from competitors and meeting a different need can the supplier improve their price position and margin."

In your search for your competitive edge, don't forget who makes you truly unique: your staff. "The one thing competitors can't quickly access is the brains of your workforce," says Susan Meisinger, former CEO of the world's leading HR organization, the Society for Human Resource Management.

In a world where technology enables competitors to quickly reverse-engineer products and services, people and the knowledge and commitment they hold remain an essential advantage. For battle-weary established businesses, constant market demands and changes can make competitive advantage harder to define and sustain. But the message is clear: even in the toughest and most crowded market where all products are alike, finding your point of difference is essential.

Jack Trout and Steve Rivkins, well-known marketing authorities on the importance of unique positioning describe in Differentiate or Die: Survival in our Era of

Killer Competition that the explosion of choice and competition has created a "cruel tyranny" where only businesses that can express their "differentness" can survive. "With enormous competition, markets are today driven by choice," they write. "The customer has so many good alternatives that you pay dearly for your mistakes. Your competitors get your business, and you don't get it back very easily. Companies that don't understand this will not survive."

If you find you're getting stale or staring at dwindling market share or profits the best and bravest step may be to stop… and dream. Says Disciplined Dreaming author Josh Linkner: "The only real sustainable competitive advantage for individuals and creativity, is creativity." Linkner believes too many businesses stop being creative read: innovative, as real-life pressures take hold. He argues that if you stay creative, you'll pursue change and continually stay ahead of the market instead of always chasing the leaders.

In fact, he recommends businesses should continuously tweak their competitive edge by devoting 5 per cent of every week to "idea time" where staff turn off their tasks and think instead of ways their company could improve its game. Hoskinson believes in the need for constant change even more strongly: "Anyone who does business the same way they did before 2008 has rocks in their head."

Having worked out your competitive advantage in the marketplace, how do you know it's right? Once again, Professor Michael Porter shows the way. He says you'll know you're getting competitive advantage right when you start posting higher profits than average for your industry. "But if all you're trying to do is essentially the same thing as your rivals, then it's unlikely that you'll ever be very successful."

If you do what everyone else's is doing but manage to do it better, you'll yield small incremental results. If you borrow from another sector completely unrelated to your business, you will have massive measurable results to show off and be proud of. Let me give you an example.

I purchased a failing pizza business that was closing due to poor management efforts, zero name brand awareness and lack of returning clients. This was a recipe for disaster, but I turned it around tremendously and ended opening up three more locations using the same marketing methodology I am about to share with you. I borrowed a slice of marketing from another business that was just crazy enough to work and it did.

At the time I acquired this single unit failing pizza place, I also owned a couple of fitness gyms where I had done very well. We increased membership 34% year over year and drastically cut our attrition rate to the low single digits while increasing net profits over 210% since my original purchase of the facilities. I eventually sold these gyms for a nice return and was overall extremely satisfied with these purchases. At this point you are probably asking yourself, "Nick where are you going with this, how is this helping me?" I say patience young grasshopper, allow yourself to continue to read.

Lets look at the three motivating and contributing factors to this pizza business failing.

1. **Poor Management:** This one was easy because we had excellent management training in place with other business that was duplicable in almost any business. Management is all people related. If you can teach someone how to read people, anticipate their needs, meet their needs before it becomes a need (that's a big one) and react appropriately to situations that will arise you'll solve the management issue. We solved this very quickly.

2. **Zero Name Brand Awareness:** Again, this one was fairly easy. What needed to be done was the guests that were coming in needed to be raving fans. They needed a reason to sell our pizzas for us through word of mouth. Nothing gets people excited to try something like a good referral from a trusted friend. But, you need to give the "friend" a reason to talk about you and "his friend" a compelling enough reason to come in. So we started a referral program. We spent a few dollars (when I mean a few I mean less then $250) to upgrade the Point of Sale system to add a Customer Relationship Management feature or what I liked to call it, the "Customer Retention Manager". I made everyone on the management staff refer to the CRM as that. I wanted to make sure people on the staff were buying into the system and why capturing clients/customers information was so important.

When someone would come in, we'd give him or her gift one, a free soda or an order of garlic knots if they checked in online making their information available to us for our marketing referral purposes. Then we would offer them gift two, if you send a friend in and they mention your name you'll receive a free large calzone. If they mention your name and check in your next pizza is on us. This gives them a compelling reason not only to tell people about us but also make sure they check in online while in the restaurant. All this certainly helped with the third challenge.

3. **Lack of Returning Clients:** This can be looked at as one of the toughest obstacles to overcome and it is if you do not understand human nature, thank goodness I do. As I stated before, if you do what everyone else is doing and do it better you will have marginal results. Basically do what everyone else is doing and be about the same, maybe a little better. But borrow from another industry where no one else is doing something similar and watch your growth quickly explode. That is exactly what I did.

As I stated I owned and successfully turned around a few fitness gyms. These were places people signed a yearly contract, paid a monthly fee and received special privileges for doing so. They received discounted and sometimes free classes they could take. The members received special passes they could give to friends and family. The members received discounts to our gym store to buy our branded workout apparel and gym bags. There were a lot of reasons to become a member.

It works for gyms, why not pizza? Oh, it works alright! I began selling monthly memberships to our pizza place. For $50 a month, you could have any pizza any time, non-delivery pickup only, limit 3 pizzas per day. Yes, theoretically one could order and pickup 90 pizza's per month for $50. The average pizza cost $1.27, if someone did order 90 pizza's in the month we would lose $64.30. Question, would you eat 90 pizzas in a month? Do you know anyone that would? Me neither, nor did anyone try to do this stunt. But, there is more to my madness. The reason it was for "pickup only" is because we wanted them to come in and buy sodas, salads, garlic knots and desserts. Human nature is predictable. When you walk in and do not have to reach in your pocket and spend money to receive a value it's easier to want to spend a few dollars on soda or salads or garlic knots. Especially when you have handed them a coupon book for these items when signing up for the monthly membership. Every time they come in they drive their own price of the membership up.

Unlike the traditional gym membership where they

wanted you to sign up for the gym and never use it, times have changed. We want you to use your membership because the more you are in the higher cost of your membership is without you even realizing it. Yes, I am a genius and yes this all works, because I've put it into action and thrived from it. It is called I win and I win because I stay up at nights designing new ways to improve my businesses while my competition is merely dreaming of a better business, a better bank account, a better life. You go ahead and sleep in your comfortable bed, take another nine hours off your day, dream about one day being better and keep giving me the advantage. Trust me, I wont waste your gift to me and when I am done, I'll live the life you only dreamt about. Sleep those little slices of death for your business and keep your life mediocre. Sweet dreams.

"Sleep that knits up the ravelled sleave of care

The death of each day's life, sore labour's bath
Balm of hurt minds, great nature's second course,

Chief nourisher in life's feast."

-William Shakespeare, *Macbeth*

You Hold the Key.

Luck, I Wouldn't Know a Damn Thing About It

"It's hard to beat a person who never gives up."

-Babe Ruth

I believe what Babe Ruth says to be true. I would also take the liberty of going one step further, I would say it is impossible to beat someone who never gives up. If they never give up then it is never over so there is never a defeat. I have lived most of my life this way. In business if something is not working we just change our approach and if that does not work then we again change our approach and if that does not work, guess what we do…change our approach again. See, we just never give up until the puzzle is figured out and we have a solid game plan for success. Our thought process is a simple one, if someone is doing it then it is possible to do, whatever it may be.

Again, I have this ego about me, I personally call it confidence, but some would argue this point and demand I say ego. Fine, I have this ego about me and the companies I create, that we always have the smartest people working for us, with us as advisors, and around us. There is nothing another company can do better than us in our space. If it is possible then I can certainly figure it out. If we cannot internally figure it out, we have the finest advisors who can assist us in doing so. We are never scared to put in the work and I find that those who claim to have all the answers stop learning, lose their edge, stop innovating and begin to fall behind.

To constantly be learning and growing is the only way to stay ahead of the curve. Being just an average company is not a goal I strive for, who wants to be average at anything? To celebrate being average or mediocre is to have given up completely on your dreams and your life. Being happy with being just as good as everyone else does not lead to a successful life. It leads to sure boredom. If you are going to get bored at something, get bored of beating everyone all the time. Then go find someone you can not beat and go try to beat them. You do not expand your life simply by beating all the same players all the time.

This is again unfulfilling, to expand you need to play people better then you. You have to have the courage to be beaten by a dominant player to get better. You do not get stronger by beating people who are not as strong or as good as you. You will end up playing to their level if you consistently play them and you will never get better. You must have the guts to play people better, faster and stronger then you currently are.

How do you build a muscle? You have to lift weights heavier then you are used to lifting. You have to lift these weights and push your body to the point of being exhausted and uncomfortable. You have to do this on a consistent basis to grow. Do you see a pattern here? If I asked you to lift that weight up and down 30 times for 30 days, do you think you would get stronger? Of course you would, but then what would happen? The weights would seem lighter over time, it would get easier to do and you might even get through the workout faster. So now what? Start lifting the weights 45 times for 30 days, that's where the growth comes in. You do not need to change the weights, all you need to do is switch up the strategy to get better, to get stronger.

Steve Jobs, may he rest in peace, understood this

application better than most everyone. Steve was demanding of his people, his time and his life. Most would not call Steve Jobs a warm and fuzzy human being, but you know what he was? He was a master of his universe. No one could tell Steve no. If they did, he basically told them to watch him do it or demand they had to figure out a way to make it happen.

When engineers were working on the very first iPod and had completed the prototype, they presented their work to Steve Jobs for his approval. Jobs played with the device, scrutinized it, weighed it in his hands, and promptly rejected it. It was too big.

The engineers explained that they had to reinvent inventing to create the iPod and that it was simply impossible to make it any smaller. Jobs was quiet for a moment. Finally he stood, walked over to an aquarium, and dropped the iPod in the tank. After it touched bottom, bubbles floated to the top.

"Those are air bubbles," he snapped. "That means there's space in there. Make it smaller."

As you read, Steve Jobs just did not take "no" or "we can not do that" or really any answer but what he believed to be true. And, if Steve thought it was true and you worked for him, then it was true. There is always a way if you are committed to find it. If you settle or just accept what is being told to you in absolute, then you are just being, what I call, a drone. A drone is someone who just does what they're told, does not try to be creative or innovate because they were not told to do so. Hear me now and believe me later, if you have to be told what to do in business, then you will quickly be out of business. We live in a time that people and industries are moving at the speed of light and you need to keep up. Waiting for someone to tell you what to do or where to go or what to say is death. You simply need to put in the work to get better.

Do you know who San Francisco native Chris Gardner is?

In *The Pursuit of Happyness,* a great movie if you haven't seen it I suggest you find time to watch it, the movie traces Christopher Gardner's journey from a homeless man to a multibillionaire. With a pearly smile on his face and the tough lines of age and experience setting base on his face, Gardner is the ultimate personification of a self-made entrepreneur, someone who refused to give up even when life was kicking him to the curb.

With no degree or experience, he managed to find himself a low-paying gig of selling medical supplies. A chance meeting with a man in a red Ferrari changed his life forever. He caught this person's attention and asked him what he did to afford such a car, to which the man replied that he was a stockbroker. Gardner often describes this as "the moment he knew" he knew that his future lay in the field of investments, strategic calculations and fat paychecks.

Lady Luck hadn't quite been favoring Gardener at this point. His girlfriend had left him and his two-year old son for a "better life" and the night before he managed to obtain an interview for an internship at San Francisco-based brokerage firm Dean Witter, he was pulled up and arrested for a night by the cops for unpaid parking tickets. Undeterred, Chris showed up for the interview in sweatpants and an undershirt from the night before. His passion and sincere urgency won him a spot in the program. But his troubles were far from over. Now homeless, Gardner struggled to find shelter. When he got lucky, he was able to find accommodation at the Glide Memorial Church Centre. But this wasn't always the case. Once, he had to sleep the night in a locked bathroom in Oakland Subway Station with his son. By the end of the internship, he was the sole trainee chosen for a permanent position at Dean Witter. A few years later, he took a position with Bear Stearns & Co., where he managed to bring in the top numbers. In 1987, he founded his own brokerage firm, Gardner Rich & Co. in Chicago, which he has since transformed into Christopher Gardner International Holdings, an institutional brokerage firm that also directs projects overseas, primarily in South Africa.

In May 2006, his memoir *The Pursuit of Happyness* was published which was soon adapted into an Academy-Award nominee film starring Will

Smith as Chris Gardner and Jaden Smith as his son, Chris Jr.

While he still runs his billion dollar firm successfully, Gardner is currently on the threshold of writing another prospective bestseller and actively involving himself in many social causes dealing with homelessness and domestic abuse. We take out a few life-changing lessons from this determined man's roller-coaster of a journey for all you motivated entrepreneurs out there.

Everyone knows that entrepreneurship is nothing without passion. If you don't feel crazy about your business or your product and you aren't staying up enthusiastically sleepless nights to go over a ten-policy program in your head for the meeting next day, then you aren't doing it right. Gardner often says that he was lucky to find a job he truly loved, one for which he couldn't wait for the sun to rise so he could get back to. Gardner didn't have any training in the job, nor did he dream of it his whole life. But he had that one instance with the red Ferrari when he knew with absolute clarity that this was what he was meant to do.

Gardner has held many interactive conferences with aspiring entrepreneurs, and one of his great pearls of advice has been "Always get your timing right." He emphasizes the importance of being at the right place at the right time, just like he was when he saw the Ferrari, or even beating bad timing, like when he had to attend the interview at Dean Witter in the same clothes he'd spent his night in jail. He advises them to be faster than time and be "aggressively early" because "being late projects the wrong image and makes people lose faith in your ability to prioritize."

Gardner has had his fair share of downs in life, and as he confesses in the book, he didn't always know how to go down the right path or make the right decision for his family. But he took the plunge anyway and made the best out of every situation, which got him to where he is now. To him, a better life can only be lived and an individual can only understand his or her true potential when they have survived a crisis they fear the most.

Today, he may carry the invisible scars of life and experience, but his shoulders lack the weight of the hopelessness they once carried because it has been replaced with something much lighter, happiness.

As with Gardner and Jobs passion moved them forward, passion kept them up at night and the true NEED to be successful is what drove them. Their need for success was driven by separate and very different reason, but the moral to these stories are large heaping's of passion, immense hard work, ridiculous work ethic and a true understanding of their "Why" is what drove them to immortality in their respective industries.

Are you ready for the sleepless nights, the never-ending work, to fight everyday for the fruits of your labor? Are you ready for the real honest hard work?

This was written by a colleague of mine Josiah Ruff, he's a motivational speaker, a lifelong hustler and a strong man who everyone can learn something from. Read this passage below from Josiah.

When it comes to success, there is rarely EVER a time when LUCK comes into play.
HARD WORK however always comes into play.

Hard Work does not offer a guarantee of success...
But without it, there is a GUARANTEE... The Guarantee of Failure!

The harder I work the luckier I get!
The harder I work the richer I get!
The harder I work the GREATER my SUCCESS!

Good things don't come to those that wait
Good things come to those that WORK HARDER THAN ALL OTHERS
GREAT things come to those that will do WHATEVER

IT TAKES
GREAT things come to those that DO THE WORK
WHEN NO-ONE IS WATCHING.

The discipline to WORK HARD...
Not when the cameras are on...
Not When the haters are watching...
But when there is no one watching, no one is caring...
When The LIGHTS ARE OFF.
How hard do you work when the lights are off?
How often do you put in work when nobody is watching?

It's in the rising early,
It's in the double and triple sessions, the extra mile, the extra hour.
It's in those little moments that the GREATS are separated from the AVERAGE.

CHAMPIONS, and SUCCESSFUL humans care not if anyone is WATCHING AT ANY MOMENT.
They care for results from their efforts.

Nothing worthwhile can be gained without hard work Indeed, It is in the greatest challenges and struggles you get your greatest satisfaction.

On the field of life there is NO SUBSTITUTE for hard work
HARD WORK BEATS talent HARD WORK BEATS luck HARD WORK BEATS EVERYTHING!
Make No Mistake!

GET THE JOB DONE!!!
Don't Look around to see if others are watching!
Don't Seek Recognition!
Don't Seek Approval!
You don't need it, and you will be better without it.

It is impossible to beat a human that doesn't give up.
It is IMPOSSIBLE to deny a human with
RELENTLESS SPIRIT to SUCCEED AT ALL COSTS!
It is Impossible to beat THE HARDEST WORKER in
the room

Work Hard until the day you no longer have to
introduce yourself
Work so hard, until ONE DAY your signature will be
called an autograph

There is NO GREATER SATISFACTION IN LIFE
THAN THAT OF HARD WORK PAYING OFF
No Greater Satisfaction Than Knowing You Are SELF
MADE.

Work hard, Play Hard, and Stay Humble

I don't want to fool you to think that anything about business is easy, because it is not. If you are in business, you have problems!

The secret is not just to learn how to solve problems, but to know which problems are most important. If you are going to be an effective leader and businessperson you have to able to separate the problem that needs your attention. You have to focus on the things that matter most because those are the decisions that are going to change your business.

There are three types of problems:

1. Normal problems, I call them the everyday, welcome to business problems. Normal problems are those that you readily encounter, solve, learn from and move on. There are normal problems that you can expect to deal with during each stage of growth.

2. Abnormal problems, these are a bit more tricky. Abnormal problems are those that you believe are solved, but that continuously reappear in a new form. These problems can trap your business in a particular stage or development and limit its ability to grow.

3. Pathological problems, these can end your business. Pathological problems are abnormal chronic problems that have extreme or dire consequences. If these problems are undetected or untreated, they can threaten the survival of an organization.

It is vital to do the right thing at the right time, especially in business. As we enter a new season of history, the most important thing any of us can do is to understand where we are now, to identify current opportunities, and ultimately to create a compelling and strategic vision of our future. Let me give you a Key Principle of business and life, you can do the right thing at the wrong time and not be rewarded.

To be fair, there are only three reasons people fail in any given situation. It all comes down to this:

1. They don't have compelling enough reasons to succeed when the going gets tough. They do not have their "Why" figured out. Perhaps you should have bigger wants out of life. Perhaps you should want to obtain your goals not for you, but for your kids to give them a better life. Maybe to retire your parents or take your entire family on a vacation. I find in life that we will do more for others than you will do for yourself. Don't you find that to be true? Lets test that theory. If you have kids, will you do more for them then you will do for yourself? Do they eat before you? Are they taken care of before you? If you are a parent, I would dare to guess the answer is yes to all the above. Perhaps you need to think of them everyday you get up and go market your business. Remember why you are really doing this.

2. They have limiting belief systems, such as: "It won't work." "I tried it before." "I've tried everything and nothing works." All these are normally complete crap they are telling themselves. When someone says to me "it won't work", I usually smile and ask why? I know I am about to listen to all their limiting beliefs about themselves, their abilities and overall their fear. Let me give you a tip when someone starts talking about their stress, because this comes up a lot with

business owners. Stress is just another way for someone who is unsuccessful to say I am scared of this or I live in fear it won't work out so I do not give it my all.

3. They don't consistently manage their state. The ability to manage your state is the difference between success and failure. When you get in your head, you are dead. To live in a consistent state of fear, you will never get what you deserve because you are constantly talking about what might happen if it doesn't work out rather then what might happen if it actually does. Crazy thought would you not agree? What if it all actually worked out, perhaps you should focus on that for a while and give yourself and your nerves a break.

"Failure is not only the punishment for laziness, there is also the success of your competitors."

-Jules Renard

If you are or were worried about failing, perhaps you should be asking yourself a few questions and be honest with yourself, no one is listening. How much money have you lost in the last three years because you haven't consistently managed your state? How much has it cost you emotionally in the last three years not to manage your state consistently? How much has it cost you in terms of frustration, pain, anger, anguish, and regret? What will it cost you over the next five years if you don't change this pattern? What would your life be like in the next five years if you consistently managed your state? What would your career be like? How much more would you enjoy yourself? How much more money would you make?

You need to make a commitment to yourself today that you will live, grow and thrive like never before. The days of old are just that, the old days, the old patterns, the old you. If you could give yourself that gift your life would change instantly. Do it now, free yourself from these limiting beliefs that have held you and your business back until now. Remember, if someone else has accomplished what you are trying to do then it can be done. Success is no accident and there is no secret formula. You just have to believe it, plan for it and work your ass off because luck, I don't know a damn thing about it.

"Nobody who ever gave his best regretted it."
–George Halas

You Hold the Key.

Responsibility

"The price of greatness is responsibility."
- Winston S. Churchill

We all have responsibilities in our lives and in this chapter, I'm going to remind you of a few history lessons and dive a bit deeper to hopefully encourage you to take this subject seriously.

Fatherhood:

Fathers have the responsibility to raise and care for a child and to take that young life and help it grow into a man of integrity. Father's are the weight and God of their child's world, whatever happens to that life is their doing.

The lit candle flickered, its deep, bright, yellow flame danced and carefully licked the side of the glass it was contained in. I lay on my bed watching the commercials drag on tediously, and I waited for the news to resume. White light from my television and computer screen cascaded over my room, creating with the candle, a flickering light. The news resumed and continued with the headliner of the dark evening. "Father kills his son." I sat up in my sheets and wondered what compels a father to do such a thing to his own son, to create a loss of life in life, and to raise a hand against his own child in such a destructive manner.

Such things make me question the quality of man. Are people really as good as we make them out to be? Who can we or I trust? Does the problem lie with the Creator? Why would He have any need for a child's wisdom, and why would He take a child like that? I strongly believe there are some things we just won't ever know nor are we supposed to understand.

Deep inside I know the problem lies in the wickedness that some people possess, but my heart breaks to think that a child can be murdered by his own father. Did his father not see the beauty and the life that he possessed? For a father to take that little innocent life and end it is unforgivable to me.

Children are the most precious thing in life. It is the reason a son leaves his mother and father, to go out and start his own family. But when a father becomes an enemy what is a child to do? We should not let children grow up too quickly. We have a responsibility to protect and love our children. We have a responsibility to teach and mold our children into productive humans. We need to teach self-respect and honor to our children because if we do not, they will learn from watching what they focus the most on. Children now days are inundated with information from all over the place; from television, the Internet, friends, strangers, and many other sources. We need to purposely intervene and make sure we are present with our children. The one thing I see on a daily basis is a parent on their phones while with their kids. They are inadvertently showing children that what they are saying is not important. This affects the value of a child, the way they see themselves and their self-respect. We have a responsibility to be present, kind, loving, and teach our children to love themselves so they can love others.

As a father of three, I know I have the responsibility to be the breadwinner, and also the leader of the house. My children will learn many things in this life, I can only hope they choose to guard their mind and learn what is good and true. I have a responsibility to not only mold their thoughts, but actually show them right from wrong. It is one thing to tell them and another to show them. Kids pay close attention and do not miss much, make sure you are on your best behavior and stay present when your kids are around. You have a responsibility to be a better person, to teach your children that life is good, and that they are here to make a positive difference in the world.

Community:

Community responsibilities are an individual's duties or obligations to the community and include cooperation, respect and participation. The concept goes beyond thinking and acting as individuals to common beliefs about shared interests and life. A basic community responsibility is voting in elections.

Each individual is part of a larger community. Family, neighbors, tribe, village, city, county, state, region, country and the world form a larger community in the life of every human being. However, full human potential cannot be reached if individuality is suppressed by society.

In all free societies there is a constant and unavoidable tension between rights and responsibilities. Every right has a corresponding duty (U.S. Department of State).

It is the responsibility of the individual to watch over a community to make sure that standards are objective and beneficial to human life (Machan 2001).

Historic Roots:

In 1787, Thomas Jefferson, the chief architect of the
Declaration of Independence, urged the drafters of the
Constitution to clearly identify the rights of the people.
Jefferson believed past governments had been harsh and
restrictive to the populace, governed questionable areas
with no just power to act no jurisdictional authority and
the result had been a reduction or loss of individual rights
(U.S. Department of State). Like Jefferson, many of the
founding fathers' generation feared the encompassing and
absolute power of a federal government and demanded a
Bill of Rights to protect the people and limit the powers
of a federal government.

The Bill of Rights contains the first ten amendments to
the United States Constitution and includes the basic
privileges of all United States citizens. Many of the rights
written in the amendments resulted from the shared
experience of both the British and the American colonists
under British rule. All the amendments reflect the close
ties between personal freedom and democracy as
versioned by the founding fathers' generation (U.S.
Department of State). Over the years, the definition of
some rights has changed and new concepts, such as
privacy were added to the Constitution. But the rights of
the people are the core of American democracy. In this
way, the United States is unique in the world; its tradition
of individual rights strongly reflects the American
experience.

Good definitions of "rights" are often lacking and subject
to interpretation. However, the Constitution provides a
mechanism for interpretation by the Supreme Court.

People may disagree with the Supreme Court regarding the meaning of a specific right, but adherence to the rules of law requires obedience to the interpretation by the Court. The justices of the Supreme Court are sworn to uphold constitutional law; their duty is to reflect and decide evolving notions or conflicts of rights. The Supreme Court is recognized as the primary agent for upholding constitutional rights and making decisions current with the needs of the time and society.

For more than two centuries, American democracy has fostered a wealth of creativity and ideas by people. Since its birth as a nation, America has been an abundant and reliable source of ideas that have empowered both individuals and communities. This characteristic was observed by Alex de Tocqueville when he visited America in 1831:

"These Americans are the most peculiar people in the world. You'll not believe it when I tell you how they behave. In a local community in their country, a citizen may conceive of some need [that] is not being met. What does he do? He goes across the street and discusses it with his neighbor. Then what happens? A committee begins functioning on behalf of that need. All of this is done by private citizens on their own initiative. The health of a democratic society may be measured by the quality of functions performed by private citizens" (Tocqueville 1956, 201).

Importance:

Citizenship today requires individuals be knowledgeable
of public problems but, more important, have the
capacity to act together toward their solutions (Morse
1989). Voluntary actions by private citizens working
together to right injustices, change directions and pursue
benefits for the common good are noted throughout
American history. This list includes the abolition of
slavery, women's suffrage, public education, community
hospitals, the civil rights movement, the women's
movement, the environmental movement, the gay rights
movement and the organization of migrant workers. In
some cases, the movements' leaders achieved great fame
and the respect of the nation and the world, such as
Martin Luther King, Jr. and Cesar Chavez. (Aviv 2003)

In every case, people voluntarily came together with a
shared sense of purpose for the common good and with
the intent of righting a wrong in the community. They
also found like-minded people of goodwill. Groups
formed alliances and multiplied their strength (Aviv
2003). In 1996, Robert Kennedy observed:

"Each time a man stands up for an ideal, or acts to
improve the lot of others, or strikes out against injustice,
he sends forth a tiny ripple of hope, and crossing each
other from a million different centers of energy and
daring, those ripples build a current which can sweep
down the mightiest walls of oppression and resistance"
(Robert F. Kennedy, former U.S. Attorney General
(1925-1968), from a speech at the Day of Affirmation at
the University of Cape Town, South Africa, June 1966).

Ties to the Philanthropic Sector:

Philanthropic people and organizations such as foundations, corporate grant makers, individual donors and workplace-giving programs generously donate time, talent and money to support the efforts and fund the success of individuals and groups struggling to resolve community problems and promote human rights.

Nonprofit charitable organizations work to identify underlying causes of social problems and effect change to benefit the public. Many significant social ideas of the past century in this country have been nurtured in the nonprofit sector (Gardner 2003). Nonprofit organizations fill gaps in areas such as social services, human rights and environmental protection. They may provide youth activities , feed the hungry, and shelter for homeless people. Nonprofit organizations reinforce both individualism and community responsibility by establishing an arena of action through which individuals can take the initiative to promote their own well-being and to advance the well-being of others in the community.

Individuals, as responsible members of their communities, may give their time and volunteer their services to help obtain needed improvements. Active participation on local school boards and parent-teacher associations improves educational services. Citizens can take an active part in the community by offering their knowledge and talents to different local organizations or committees. Participation in town meetings, public hearings and community projects is important for community improvement and identifying and solving problems.

Important People Related to the Topic:

President Thomas Jefferson: President Jefferson drafted the Declaration of Independence in 1776, which proved to be the defining event in his life and legacy to the nation. Drawing on documents, such as the Virginia Declaration of Rights, state and local calls for independence and his own draft of a Virginia constitution, Jefferson wrote a stunning and eloquent statement of the colonists' right to rebel against the British government. It decreed the colonists' independence and right to self-government, based on the premise all men are created equal and have the unalienable rights to life, liberty and the pursuit of happiness (Library of Congress 2002).

President Abraham Lincoln: President Lincoln issued the Emancipation Proclamation on September 22, 1862, as the United States was embattled and divided by the start of the third year of the Civil War. The proclamation became effective on January 1, 1863. The historic document freed all slaves in the country, including slaves in rebelling confederate states that endorsed secession from the Union. Lincoln mandated enforcement of the proclamation by the Union military. Issuance and enforcement of the Emancipation Proclamation nearly cost President Lincoln his presidency; it may have cost his life. His courage and wisdom paved the way for the passage of the13th Amendment to the Constitution (December 1865), which ended slavery in the United States.

Elizabeth Cady Stanton met **Susan B. Anthony** in 1851 and for the next fifty years worked in close collaboration; Stanton articulated arguments for the improvement of women's legal and traditional rights ; Anthony organized and campaigned to achieve these goals (The Anthony Center 2002).

Andrew Carnegie: Carnegie was perhaps the first wealthy man to state publicly the rich have a moral obligation to give away their fortunes. In 1889 he wrote *The Gospel of Wealth,* in which he asserted all personal wealth beyond that required to supply the needs of one's family should be regarded as a trust fund to be administered for the benefit of the community (Carnegie Corporation of New York).

Rosa Parks: Parks refused to give up her seat to a white man on a bus in Montgomery, Alabama in 1955, an action regarded as the beginning of the U.S. Civil Rights Movement. "When I declined to give up my seat, it was not that day or bus in particular," Parks later told a biographer. "I just wanted to be free, like everybody else" (Hamilton 2003).

Dr. Martin Luther King, Jr.: King led a mass struggle for racial equality that changed America . King's address "I Have a Dream" delivered on the occasion of the March on Washington for Civil Rights on August 28, 1963, is one of the best-known American speeches of the twentieth century. In 1983, President Ronald Reagan signed legislation naming a federal holiday honoring King's birthday on the third Monday of every January.

Cesar Chavez: Chavez successfully represented the labor rights of farm workers, particularly Latino and

Filipino, who suffered substandard wages and working conditions. In the 1960s and 1970s, his grassroots organization ballooned into a national movement; several campaigns, including a grape boycott, were observed by more than 17 million Americans (Cauldron 2002). Mr. Chavez had a powerful impact on the plight of hired and migrant agricultural workers and on public awareness of the workers. In the years following the boycotts, federal legislation and laws in many states were enacted to provide better wages, working conditions, education and housing.

Personal Responsibility:

Ancient Romans understood the concept of personal responsibility. After a Roman arch was completed, the engineer who built it had to stand underneath it when the scaffolding was removed. While a giant arch might not crush you if you make mistakes, you still have personal responsibility for your actions. What is personal responsibility? It is taking conscious control of your responses to the events and circumstances in your life.

You *are* responsible for yourself, whether you like it or not. What you do with your life and what you have done already is up to you. "But Nick! Things happen to me that I have no control over all the time!" Sure. And while you may not be able to control everything that happens to you, you are nevertheless responsible for how you think, act, and feel in response to those things.

Responsibility cannot be split. If you "give" someone else any of the responsibility, you take it off yourself and can use it as an excuse to slack off when the going gets rough. Do you think the engineers in ancient Rome shared responsibility for their creations? Traditionally, we have viewed the notion of responsibility in a negative way; it is a matter of obligation or of having duties. I will argue, accepting personal responsibility for your life is actually quite liberating.

Trust And Respect From Other People:

Let's say you make a mistake while working on a project at work. If you admit your mistake, people are more likely to believe you about other things you do. Your word has more meaning to other people when you take responsibility. But it's not just a matter of trust. You also earn lots of respect when you take responsibility for your actions.

It is rare for someone to willingly and without hesitation fess up for their mistakes, so when you do, you will stick out. If you develop a reputation for being the guy who accepts responsibility for his actions, people will often simply ignore the fact that you made a mistake altogether.

Fewer Negative Emotions:

There are all sorts of negative emotions that come with

not accepting personal responsibility. When you blame others, you may feel anger or resentment towards that person. You will almost invariably feel guilty or ashamed. The worst part about denying responsibility is an overall sense of powerlessness. When you feel like you don't have control over your life, you can easily become depressed.

How To Take Responsibility For Your Life:

You need to make a conscious decision to become the sole person responsible for your life, and you need to make that decision now. But you can't just say you've decided to take personal responsibility and then have it be true. Surrendering responsibility is a habit that you need to remove, and here is how.

Recognize Your Choices:

At any given time and in any given situation, you have a choice of how to respond. It doesn't matter how terrible your circumstances are. You could be locked away in a prison, but you still control your mental state. You can choose to focus on something positive, no matter how negative a situation you are in. From now on, look at the choices you have available to you instead of feeling constrained.

Take The Blame:

When something goes wrong, openly acknowledge it as your fault, even if you feel there were external circumstances that contributed. If you shift responsibility to someone or something else, you will remain stuck in a rut because "it's _____'s fault!" It doesn't matter whose fault it is. When you shift responsibility, you give up control of the situation.

Don't be afraid to take risks or make important decisions. Don't be afraid to mess up, even though it can be "scary" to take responsibility for your actions. It's even scarier what you may have missed by acting out of fear. So, when there is a problem, don't ask yourself who is to blame. Instead, ask yourself: "What could I have done differently?" This shifts the focus onto your control of the situation instead of feeling like a victim.

Accept Yourself And Your Circumstances:

Accept responsibility for who you are right now. It's not other people who made you the way you are, but only your own thoughts and actions. Sure, your family, society, friends, or any other external influence conditioned many of those thoughts and actions in you, but it is you alone who had the thought or performed the action. And it is you alone who must take responsibility for them. You don't need to be happy with your situation or your life as it is, you just need to accept yourself and the fact that you are the one who got yourself there.

While negative circumstances may have had a significant impact on you and you may have experienced huge amounts of social conditioning, dwelling on them or blaming others won't help you improve your situation. Only through accepting personal responsibility can you move forward.

Stop Relying On External Validation:

Don't depend on other people to feel good about yourself. If you need external validation to be happy, you surrender personal responsibility for making yourself happy. Sure, external validation is pleasant, and there is nothing wrong with that, but you cannot be *dependent* on it for your happiness. Learn to validate yourself through acting authentically to your own values. This way you are in total control of your own happiness, because it is solely based on the way you act.

Be Open To New Ideas And Beliefs:

You should be constantly challenging your own beliefs and filters through which you view the world.
Your limiting beliefs make it significantly more challenging to take personal responsibility. If you think that unless you have the body of a model you won't get laid, you are making an excuse for your failure in a particular area. You lose motivation to do anything about it.

Forgive Yourself And Others:

People make mistakes. It's inevitable. You do it. Other people do it. Everyone does. You must learn to both forgive yourself and to forgive other people for any mistakes. If you mess up, don't beat yourself up over it. Just take responsibility and move on. When someone else messes up, don't hold it against them. If you hold on to blame, then you are shifting the focus away from your own personal responsibility for your life.

You Are Not Responsible For Other People:

Accepting personal responsibility involves letting go of the need to feel responsible for others. Everybody is responsible for himself or herself, whether they realize it or not. If you feel burdened by other people, you need to let go of them. It isn't your duty to take care of them, just as it isn't their duty to look after you.

Throughout history we have been taught time and time over that one needs to take responsibility for their actions, their values, and their lives. Remember the buck stops with you and you alone can change your life for the better at any moment. Just take the responsibility for it and live a life of true fulfillment.

In closing, this is the time in the book when I am going to tell you, "enough is enough." You don't owe me, you don't owe your family and you don't owe your community as much as you owe you to be great. Stop the excuses, get to work and expect more out of yourself than anyone else possibly could. A life of fulfillment doesn't come easily, and success is never free. Make your future-self proud by starting today, to no longer accept the limitations you have put on yourself or the crippling story you have created and accepted to be true. Make the end of this book, the beginning of the rest of your life. Be extremely proud, and very excited for what comes next. Life is beautiful.

"Attack the evil that is within yourself, rather than attacking the evil that is in others."

- Confucius

You Hold the Key.

ABOUT THE AUTHOR

Nick-Anthony Zamucen is a three time published author, business strategist and an award winning serial entrepreneur. He has had tremendous success in various business ventures which span across many diverse ventures. Nick-Anthony is a true visionary and interrupter of traditional business methodologies.

Through his own experience, Nick-Anthony Zamucen has realized that one of his greatest strengths was assisting other people's success. A core belief of Nick-Anthony's is "Success breeds Success". For this reason, Nick-Anthony has assembled an elite "success group" based around business franchising and peak performance coaching . He has created some of the most intensive, informative, and educational success forums in the world.

Apart from Nick's dedication to his family and career, he is equally invested in his philanthropic efforts. 10 years ago, Nick-Anthony Zamucen started a 501(c) called Project Penny Pickup, which supports his initiative to help nourish the homeless in San Francisco. Nick has also been actively involved with Feeding America, a nationwide nonprofit supporting similar efforts. Nick-Anthony is a firm believer in helping where help is needed, which is why a fundamental value of his is "Help First, Everything Else Second".

Made in the USA
Las Vegas, NV
19 March 2022

45963815R00100